D0006473

Guide to

Media Relations

37653010146986
Terry   NonFiction
659.2 SCHENKLER
Guide to media relations

CENTRAL ARKANSAS LIBRARY SYSTEM
ADOLPHINE FLETCHER TERRY
BRANCH LIBRARY
LITTLE ROCK, ARKANSAS

FEB - - 2004

Prentice Hall Series
in Advanced Business Communication

Guide to

Media Relations

Irv Schenkler
Stern School of Business
New York University

Tony Herrling
Burson-Marsteller, Inc.
Public Relations/Public Affairs

PEARSON
Prentice
Hall

Upper Saddle River, New Jersey 07458

Library of Congress Cataloging-in-Publication Data

Schenkler, Irv.
  Guide to media relations / Irv Schenkler, Tony Herrling.
    p. cm.—(Prentice Hall series in advanced communication)
  Includes bibliographical references and index.
  ISBN 0-13-140567-5 (pbk. : alk. paper)
    1. Public relations. 2. Mass media and business I. Herrling, Tony. II. Title. III. Series.

HD59.S327 2003
659.2—dc21   2003046381

Acquisitions Editor: David Parker
Vice President/Editor-in-Chief: Jeff Shelstad
Assistant Editor: Ashley Keim
Editorial Assistant: Melissa Yu
Marketing Manager: Shannon Moore
Senior Managing Editor (Production): Judy Leale
Production Assistant: Joseph DeProspero
Associate Director, Manufacturing: Vincent Scelta
Production Manager: Arnold Vila
Manufacturing Buyer: Diane Peirano
Cover Design: Kiwi Design
Cover Illustration/Photo: Kiwi Design
Composition/Full-Service Project Management: Rainbow Graphics/Linda Begley
Printer/Binder: Phoenix

Credits and acknowledgments borrowed from other sources and reproduced, with permission, in this textbook appear on appropriate pages within text.

Copyright © 2004 by Pearson Education, Inc., Upper Saddle River, New Jersey, 07458.
Pearson Prentice Hall. All rights reserved. Printed in the United States of America. This
publication is protected by Copyright and permission should be obtained from the publisher prior to any prohibited reproduction, storage in a retrieval system, or transmission in
any form or by any means, electronic, mechanical, photocopying, recording, or likewise.
For information regarding permission(s), write to: Rights and Permissions Department.

Pearson Prentice Hall™ is a trademark of Pearson Education, Inc.
Pearson® is a registered trademark of Pearson plc
Prentice Hall® is a registered trademark of Pearson Education, Inc.

Pearson Education LTD.   Pearson Education Australia PTY, Limited
Pearson Education Singapore, Pte. Ltd   Pearson Education North Asia Ltd
Pearson Education, Canada, Ltd   Pearson Educación de Mexico, S.A. de C.V.
Pearson Education–Japan   Pearson Education Malaysia, Pte. Ltd

10 9 8 7 6 5 4 3 2 1
ISBN 0-13-140567-5

CENTRAL ARKANSAS LIBRARY SYSTEM
ADOLPHINE FLETCHER TERRY BRANCH
LITTLE ROCK, ARKANSAS

Contents

CHAPTER IV

COUNT THE CATCH:
DEALING WITH THE FINANCIAL MEDIA

CHAPTER V

BATTEN DOWN THE HATCHES:
HANDLING THE MEDIA IN A CRISIS

BIBLIOGRAPHY

INDEX

Introduction

HOW THIS BOOK CAN HELP YOU

This book is a practical guide to media relations. If you need to know how to work with and communicate effectively with the media, this book can help you to:

- Identify important media contacts
- Establish ongoing relationships with reporters
- Prepare for media interviews
- Write press releases and plan press conferences
- Create a press list
- Communicate with the financial media
- Manage media relations during a crisis

If you also are interested in a more general discussion about the relationship between business and the media, this book can help you to:

- Understand the nature of today's media
- Assess how market forces affect media coverage
- Understand how reporters conceive stories
- Differentiate between financial media and mainstream media
- Analyze the nature of media coverage in a crisis
- Review a range of strategies for responding to crises

WHO CAN USE THIS BOOK

This book was written for you if you work in a business or not-for-profit organization and want (1) to understand what motivates reporters and how to convey your organization's messages to them, (2) to learn more about the media's pervasive presence in and influence on business, (3) to learn about the techniques of effective media communication, and/or (4) to take charge of media relationships and better assess the dynamics of media interaction. Specifically, this book is written for . . .

- *Anyone who may be involved in a business crisis:* The book dissects crisis communication and details a set of strategic responses to crises.
- *Those who are new to media relations:* The book provides an overview of the primary channels you can use to reach the media and offers insights into reporters' methods.
- *Those already in the field:* The book presents additional ways to sell your stories to the media and engage reporters' interest.
- *General managers of companies and principals of start-ups:* The book details how you can improve your programs to communicate with the financial press.
- *Executives who oversee their companies' communication functions:* The book offers insights about maintaining corporate and business reputations—the fundamental reason for effective media strategy.
- *MBA students who want to learn about the media:* The book will help future managers who may find themselves interacting with the media.

WHY THIS BOOK WAS WRITTEN

Over the course of 20 years, the many professionals and students we have encountered—either while consulting to organizations, teaching at New York University's Stern School of Business, or working with clients as a Managing Director for Burson-Marsteller, one of the world's largest public relations firms—have told us of the need for a concise summary of media relations. These busy professionals have found other books on this subject either too long or too simplistic for their needs. That's why Prentice Hall is publishing the Prentice Hall Series in Advanced Business Communication—brief, practical, reader-friendly guides for those who communicate in professional contexts. (See the inside front cover for more information on the series.)

- *Brief:* This book summarizes key ideas only. Culling from thousands of pages of text and research, we have omitted bulky examples, cases, footnotes, exercises, and discussion questions.

- *Practical:* This book offers clear, straightforward tools you can use. It includes only information that you will find useful in a professional context.

- *Reader-friendly:* We have tried to provide an easy-to-skim format—using a direct, matter-of-fact, nontheoretical tone.

HOW THIS BOOK IS ORGANIZED

This book is divided into five chapters:

Chapter I: Setting Your Media Strategy   explains what drives the media today, and defines your primary channels (such as press releases, interviews, etc.) to communicating with them.

Chapter II: Developing Proactive Media Relations   explains how to (1) develop a newsworthy message, (2) get to know reporters and attract their interest in your story, (3) use media channels effectively, and (4) engage public relations agencies.

Chapter III: Responding to Media Calls   explains how to prepare for and effectively execute media interviews—when the media comes to you.

Chapter IV: Dealing with Financial Media Relations   explains how to (1) issue financial news such as quarterly earnings and executive changes, and (2) communicate your messages about transformational events such as mergers and acquisitions or restructurings.

Chapter V: Handling the Media in a Crisis   (1) explains why the media covers corporate crises, (2) provides strategies a company can use to handle the media during crises, and (3) offers tactical advice for dealing with reporters during crises.

ACKNOWLEDGMENTS

We acknowledge the many people who made this book possible.

I'd like to thank the many professionals from public relations and the media who generously took time over the years to guest lecture in my courses at New York University, including Chris Atkins, Jeff Bloch, Claudia Deutsch, Joe Fitzgerald, Richard Hyde, Jim Horton, Robert Mead, and Leslie-Gaines Ross. Paul Argenti provided thoughtful comments on the manuscript. My wife, Lynn Russell, offered extensive advice; the book is all the better for her essential assistance. And I'd like to acknowledge the best communicator I know, our cat, Martini, whose effective use of communication channels enables him to awaken us every morning, earlier than we wish but according to his desire. (*I.S.*)

There isn't enough space on the page to acknowledge all those colleagues, clients, analysts, reporters, and friends who have helped make this book, or the knowledge that supports it, possible. But I would especially honor the memories of my old boss Rufus Crater, New York Bureau Chief of Broadcasting Magazine (and a damned good newspaperman), and J. Garrett Blowers, whom I knew as VP, Investor Relations, CBS Inc., in appreciation of the wisdom and encouragement they shared during my own years in journalism. Thanks as well to my wife, Jane Haburay, neighbor Carol Glaws, and friends John and Sandy Barbo, for always asking, "How's the book coming along?" And finally, special thanks to my daughter Eliza Jane—from whom I learn new things every day. (*A.H.*)

Irv Schenkler
Stern School of Business
New York University

Tony Herrling
Burson-Marsteller
Public Relations/Public Affairs

Guide to

Media Relations

CHAPTER 1 OUTLINE

I. Understanding the media in general
   1. What motivates the media?
   2. What types of stories do they write?
   3. What venues do they use?
   4. How do they approach their task?

II. Analyzing your channels to the media
   1. Using press releases—the common denominator
   2. Targeting individual media outlets
   3. Targeting broad media audiences

CHAPTER I

Plot Your Course: Setting Your Media Strategy

oday, the demand for business news commands an increasingly vibrant market. As a result, stories that once would have been ignored are now the focal point of public interest. A CEO's salary, accounting irregularities, or a company's exposure to volatile markets—stories that used to put audiences to sleep—today raise eyebrows as more people take direct responsibility for their investments.

The business of business has become news in a startling way: what was once considered irrelevant to economic reporting has now found its way into the daily press. "I think business people have become general interest celebrities," says *New York Times* veteran correspondent Claudia Deutsch: "The bar has been lowered. Readers are interested in how business people are spending their money and living their lives."

As reports of corporate misconduct have become rife, business has been drawn into the media spotlight. When the general public sees a connection between its financial well-being and the actions of the business community, the media will both drive and respond to this interest. As a result, today people want to know how businesses operate and what makes them "tick." For companies, this change in the nature of business reporting becomes vital for two reasons.

The media can affect reputation.   Corporate reputation can be defined as the overall impression a company makes on its key stakeholders, from employees to investors to customers. The media are important because they influence reputation. They can have a positive influence—which is why companies inundate the media with press releases when they have good news. They can also have a negative influence—which is why some companies try to hide from media attention.

The media provide the conduit to important audiences.   For any organization, the media provide a conduit to the organization's real audiences. The media can be the most direct and most available channel to: (1) reach the customers who buy a company's products and services, (2) influence the opinions of elected officials and regulators, (3) help motivate employees who read or listen to stories about their company, (4) convey financial information to investors, and (5) enhance and defend corporate reputation.

This chapter examines the nature of today's media and then defines the range of communication channels available for you to deal with the media.

I. UNDERSTANDING THE MEDIA IN GENERAL

Who are "the media?" The phrase is a catchall that covers a lot of territory: (1) Television news programs like *60 Minutes* and your local station's *Live at Five* newscasts are some of the first things that come to mind. (2) Major newspapers of national significance, like the *New York Times*, *USA Today*, the *Wall Street Journal*, and the *Washington Post,* certainly factor into consideration. (3) Magazines also merit attention. Newsstands display everything from major news weeklies (such as *Time* or *Newsweek*), to the major business magazines (*Forbes*, *Fortune*, and *BusinessWeek*) to hundreds of special interest consumer magazines. (4) Closer to home, "the media" also include your local suburban weekly newspaper (more than 9,000 of them can be found in America) and local radio news and call-in programs. (5) It's also increasingly important to think of certain websites as media that have influence. (6) Finally, don't forget business and trade publications. According to *Bacon's Information*, a leading media directory service, more than 6,600 trade and business publications exist in the United States.

Some observers have expressed concern about the emergence of media conglomerates. A number of them—AOL Time Warner, Bertlesman, Condé Nast, Disney, News Corp., and Viacom among them—are said to constitute a threat to the diversity of available opinion and viewpoints. An FCC (Federal Communication Commission) report released in October 2002, highlights several important trends. It confirms that in ten U.S. media markets (including both small and large metropolitan areas), media outlet ownership has recently consolidated. It also notes that significant growth has occurred over the past two decades in the number of radio stations, TV stations, daily newspapers, and average number of cable channels that serve these markets. The report concludes: "The percent increase in the number of outlets averaged almost 200 percent across all ten markets."

This vast and still growing web of mass communications sources, some fiercely independent, others part of large media chains, together comprise today's media. A common thread unites them all—how they portray your organization or industry will be vital to its economic health.

1. What motivates the media?

Journalism is market driven. The media respond to audience interest and strive to sell stories. These stories may range from industry-wide exposés to CEO profiles—the reporter's interest may be salacious or high-minded—but all stories share one common denominator: they must attract "eyes" or the media outlet will go out of business.

Understanding today's media: The media aren't there simply to sell your products or services or just to reprint your press releases. They have a job to do, too.

- *They want to gain their audience's interest.* Readers and viewers want information from the media. Often, important information has a negative cast, which leads many business executives to ask, "Why are 'the media' always so negative?" Stories about "negative" topics such as defective products are news because they provide information that interests the audience. Such stories are nothing new: as far back as a hundred years ago, a group of American journalists known as "The Muckrakers" made headlines by castigating "Big Business." Their stories interested readers, sold enormous numbers of newspapers and magazines, and made fortunes for their publishers.

- *They may want to entertain their audience.* Often underestimated is the media's desire to entertain their audience. This impulse can take varying forms because the makeup of the particular audience will dictate the nature of the appeal. For example, some individuals or businesses manage to exist in a halo of positive mention (often for a limited time) and become "darlings of the press." The media often bestow upon them adulation and uncritical coverage. That positive attitude can, in fact, become contagious, and insulate a company from deeper analysis. It mirrors the process of "celebrity"—feeding the public's appetite for a constant flow of information about popular individuals in the arts, sports, and entertainment. But "the public"—and "the media"—can be fickle. Once the tide turns, the once-fawning paparazzi can become a shark pack.

More than one company has found itself in the midst of a media-induced frenzy. The box on the next page illustrates the fate of one such company and how coverage of it veered from one extreme to the other.

ENRON AND MEDIA COVERAGE

A classic example of the contrast between positive and negative coverage can be found in the reporting on ENRON, the energy company that collapsed in 2001 from the weight of scandals about questionable accounting practices.

In earlier days, ENRON had seemed to many, not just in the media but in the financial community and in the power industry, to be an exciting, entrepreneurial company, a scrappy newcomer breathing fresh air into the stale and cumbersome power businesses. Typical headlines about ENRON were:

Slam Dunk for Enron
Experts Pick: Enron
Enron Redefines Utility Industry

Once the tide turned, the headlines changed:

Enron Energy Deals Run Out of Gas
Enron Scandal Brings Overdue Scrutiny
Short Circuit: How Enron's Plan Fizzled

Note the role that the media played in uncovering what is generally accepted as a massive failure of business accountability. It was not the government regulators charged with overseeing energy companies, not the accountants who had a responsibility to review and approve ENRON financial statements, nor anyone else who burst this bubble. Instead, a mid-level reporter for *Fortune*, assigned to file a "boring" story on corporate accounting practices, persisted in asking the questions that ultimately led to unraveling the ENRON web.

Assessing political motivations: While many people accuse the media of a "liberal" bias—and some studies do suggest that members of mainstream news organizations skew toward the Democratic Party as opposed to the Republican Party—there are increasingly more visible examples of "conservative" commentary and perspective in the mainstream media. For example, commentators with conservative leanings can be found on National Public Radio—considered by its critics to be a hotbed of "liberal" media sentiment. As another example, FOX News regularly draws fire from those who feel it departs from the once sacred path of journalistic "objectivity" to promote a conservative point of view.

More compelling than that anecdotal evidence is the result of an academic study conducted in 1998 by David Croteau for the national media watch group FAIR (Fairness and Accuracy in the Media), concluding that:

- Journalists are mostly centrist in their political orientation.
- The minority of journalists who do not identify with the "center" are more likely to identify with the "right" when it comes to economic issues and to identify with the "left" when it comes to social issues.
- On select issues from corporate power and trade to Social Security and Medicare to health care and taxes, journalists are actually more conservative than the general public.
- Journalists believe that "business-oriented news outlets" and "major daily newspapers" provide the highest-quality coverage of economic policy issues, while "broadcast network TV news" and "cable news services" provide the worst.

2. What types of stories do they write?

News stories usually fall into three distinct categories: (1) breaking news, (2) feature stories, and (3) commentary. Knowing what these stories entail can be helpful either when you want to contribute information on behalf of your organization or when you are asked to provide answers to a reporter. Chapter II explains how you can tailor your message to a media outlet and Chapter III discusses how you can best respond when the media come calling on you.

Breaking news: As events transpire, reporters will be obtaining information from sources familiar with the situation, experts in the subject, governmental authorities, or eyewitnesses. Wire services, such as the Associated Press or Bloomberg, provide reporters with ongoing information. Some of this information may be inaccurate or incomplete, particularly if the story is developing and complex in nature. Often, reporters must juggle their sources and assess the validity of the raw data as they put together breaking news stories. When their deadline approaches—the time when their story must be filed for publication or broadcast—reporters will work feverishly to tie loose ends and complete their submissions.

Feature stories: These articles or broadcasts allow for greater depth and development than do breaking news. They may be profiles, exposés, new-product announcements, or medical breakthroughs. Feature stories can provide companies with a way to reach key constituencies. (Chapter II offers insights into how you can contribute to such stories.) While reporters will face deadlines on these kinds of pieces, usually there will be more time available for them to put together a feature than would be the case in breaking news. In broadcast media, however, feature stories may have a short development period or a reporter may be rushing to put together several features simultaneously.

Commentary: Usually reserved for senior reporters who have covered a field for many years or who are considered an expert, the commentary story may accompany a breaking news article to provide context. Commentaries, however, are not the same as columns; most columns are written by journalists who no longer cover a subject on a day-to-day basis (although there are exceptions). Columns occur regularly and may command a loyal following. Commentaries, by contrast, are usually linked to news stories.

3. What venues do they use?

Journalists working in different types of media operate with different parameters. Getting a sense of these parameters can help you when you need to convey information or when you are asked to respond about an issue involving your organization.

Daily papers: Dailies are generally written for that day's deadline—usually no later than 5:30 or 6:00 P.M. (A rare exception these days is the few remaining afternoon papers—midmorning is their close for comment.) Miss that deadline in returning a call and you'll find the phrase, "the company could not be reached for comment" in the story. As you approach the deadline, there will be less opportunity for you to influence, or in some cases to even appear in, the story. But then that might be your objective: to be in time to have your response included in the final story. But not so early that you provide greater opportunity for an in-depth probe or for further comment from your opposition.

Weekly publications: These weeklies have more time and compose on different schedules. There will still be deadlines but they are usually several days from the first inquiry—which can provide you additional time to ponder the questions and devise answers.

Television and radio: Both want to tell their stories in "sound bites," pithy phrases that can capture the essence of a point and sound entertaining. Their reports are generally short—unless it's an investigative piece—and their production timetables have to allow for transmission back to the studio, where scripts are prepared to accompany raw tape and the piece is edited before the broadcast. Anyone interacting with broadcast journalists should know how individual programs are scheduled, including the length of the show and its segments.

Internet news sites: These sites are frequently working off the media outlets' primary news desks. For example, most national newspapers with Internet sites will reproduce the day's hard copy stories electronically and run news wire service stories for updates. Although the same can be said for many television or radio stations with Internet links, new technologies are moving these media toward electronic convergence. It is now possible to see or hear reports on the World Wide Web, and though many features may be recycled, they can be updated to reflect changes in breaking news.

4. How do they approach their task?

Some people joke that there are no new ideas for the media—they simply keep recycling one anothers' ideas. But that jab isn't far from the truth. For example, a prominently positioned article in a national newspaper may turn up in a network newsmagazine broadcast two weeks later. A morning tabloid feature on a local issue may find its way to the evening's local "action news." The modified report may be somewhat different than the original version but the underlying story will be the same.

Topic development: Although each media outlet has its own procedures, we can make a number of generalizations about the source of news and feature stories. They are:

- assigned by editors,
- proposed by reporters, or
- pitched by interested outsiders hoping to promote their companies, products, or industries.

The inverted pyramid: Once they have crystallized a topic, reporters construct their stories by using a pattern called "the inverted pyramid." All reporters, editors, and broadcast news producers know they are competing for the audience's attention. Interest has to be captured immediately—in the headline or first sentence of a story, or in the opening seconds or initial image of a broadcast news report. So in news reporting, the "big idea" goes first, followed perhaps by some meaty quotes and context. Supporting detail follows at the end—where individual facts can be easily cut out if there's not enough time or space in today's news hole.

II. ANALYZING YOUR CHANNELS TO THE MEDIA

Once you understand the media in general, think about the broad array of channels you can use to communicate your stories to them. These channels range from soft-sell approaches (intended to plant an idea with a single reporter), to major events, (designed to communicate vital information rapidly and capture broad media attention). These channels fall into three main groups, which are discussed here: (1) press releases, (2) individually targeted channels, and (3) broadly targeted channels. The following section discusses how to use these channels as part of your proactive media relations program.

1. Using press releases—the common denominator

One of the most versatile channels at your disposal is the press release. This multipurpose document is a page or more of text that formally announces your news, your new product, or even your disaster. Releases can range from soft feature items, which do little more than keep your company's name in front of the media, to statements of financial performance, which are official documents in the eyes of government regulators.

Every release is written to mirror the way a newspaper might report your story, introduced by a catchy headline before getting to the "meat" of the subject. The process of writing the press release, and getting it approved, forces you to focus on your key messages and make them easily understood.

The press release is perhaps the most widely used channel for connecting with reporters. Although some releases will target specific media, most will be used more broadly for general outreach. However, they are not without their drawbacks. Some of the advantages and disadvantages of this channel include:

- *Advantages:* A press release (1) lets you create the story the way you want it to be read; (2) puts all your key messages in a readily understood format; (3) uses a format that journalists instantly recognize, one that is tailored to their needs; and (4) forms a permanent record that can be archived to show the history of a product or concept.

- *Disadvantages:* A press release also (1) leaves a paper trail that can come back to haunt the unwary, for example, as proof of a promise not met; (2) gets lost in the flurry of other releases that inundate reporters and editors; and (3) misses the mark if poorly conceived or written and, in such cases, may even detract from your message or annoy the reporter.

2. Targeting individual media outlets

In addition to using general press releases, you may want to target individual reporters. These contacts may range from informal, personal outreach to more formal yet individually targeted events.

Pitch letters and follow-up calls: A tried-and-true method of getting your story to individual reporters is the "pitch letter," a communiqué that attempts to make your case in a more conversational tone than a press release—and serves as the trigger for a follow-up call. "Letter" itself is an outdated term. Conventional mail is almost never used to deliver pitch letters anymore. These days, even the fax—just a short while ago the favored delivery system for print materials— has been supplanted by email.

Like the press release, this channel has advantages and disadvantages associated with it:

- *Advantages:* Pitch letters (1) personalize your contact with a reporter and show that you are familiar with his or her work and interests and (2) lead to a productive dialogue when they are well crafted and based on proper research.

- *Disadvantages:* On the other hand, pitch letters (1) require extensive preparation since you need to review the journalist's past coverage and compare how similar stories have been treated (such effort may not be justified for every story), and (2) can get lost in the reporter's or editor's email system unless the subject line grabs attention.

Email: As a vehicle for everything from transmitting press releases and pitch letters to responding to a reporter's inquiry or maintaining dialogue, email is replacing the fax and the telephone for many communicators.

- *Advantages:* (1) Email is in step with the pace of our broadband age. Technology reporters live and die by email. (2) It can provide a more comfortable level of "distance" than does the telephone. (3) It also leaves a record, which can be invaluable in resolving misunderstandings.

- *Disadvantages:* (1) Email, poorly executed, can get in the way of real communication because it encourages some of the worst tendencies of poor writing: run-on sentences, incomplete thoughts, and general verbosity. (2) Email simply doesn't work for some journalists who don't want to join the technology revolution. (3) Messages can get lost in the "spam" that afflicts the in-boxes of every email user. (4) Email leaves a record, perhaps documenting comments that shouldn't have been put in writing.

Social conversations: Lunch, breakfast, cocktails, and parties remain an important part of the mythology of "schmoozing" the press. However, reporters today are increasingly busy, and may not be inclined to spend two hours out of the office without a solid purpose; they've got too many other things to be writing or phoning about. Also, some publications, to make sure they don't give even the appearance of impropriety, have policies that require reporters to refuse to accept gifts—and a fancy lunch would count as such. But where feasible, breakfasts, lunches, and a range of other semisocial occasions can be helpful ways to create a framework for long-term, ongoing contact with a reporter. Indeed, entertainment, fashion, sports, and other businesses rely on parties, premieres, and other quasi-social occasions to ensure that they stay in the limelight.

- *Advantages:* Social conversations (1) help communicate "personality" and the other intangible qualities; (2) provide low-key opportunities to plant the seed of a story idea subtly, which you can explore further down the road; and (3) offer a sense of privacy and privilege, since you singled out a specific reporter for special attention.

- *Disadvantages:* However, social conversations (1) lead to a quagmire of informality, with more than one executive regretting an offensive remark or premature detail that "slipped out" during an informal conversation lubricated with one too many martinis; and (2) require further follow-up to ensure that the reporter won't forget or ignore that little morsel of information you so skillfully tried to plant.

Desk-side chats: In today's world of crowded schedules and lean newsroom staffs, most reporters don't have the luxury of attending all the events presented for their consideration. However, if you are willing to make things convenient for them, many will clear time on their schedules to let you stop by their offices and make your pitch. In practice, reporters will typically find a conference room for the meeting or at least suggest you conduct the visit over coffee in the company cafeteria.

- *Advantages:* Desk-side chats (1) convey a subtle acknowledgment of the news organization's importance to your company, which is why you're willing to go to them; and (2) save the reporter time and effort so you gain extra attention to the details of your story.

- *Disadvantages:* Desk-side chats also (1) challenge corporate egos, since your senior executives may feel their elevated status demands that reporters come to them; and (2) take place in an informal environment that can lead you and your team to a false sense of security.

One-on-one interviews: The most direct and potentially unnerving channel to the media is the formal interview. These interviews can be done in person—typically in your own office, though sometimes in a broadcast studio or a "neutral" location—or conducted over the phone.

Because the most delicate interviews are those associated with reactive media experiences (times when the media seek comment from you on a story that they are developing), the theory and practice of interviews are covered extensively in Chapter III. In situations when you are pitching a story to the media, the telephone interview is generally your workhorse for providing details and first-person comments. It may also be the channel you choose when circumstances dictate fast, personal media outreach on breaking news.

- *Advantages:* (1) Telephone interviews give you a high level of control over who speaks to whom and also allow for easy scheduling, with executives often able to work from the convenience of their own offices. (2) In addition, in-person interviews can effectively convey the intangibles of personality.
- *Disadvantages:* (1) Telephone interviews lack many nonverbal elements, which means that your words are more likely to be misinterpreted. (2) Both phone and in-person interviews connect you to only a single media outlet—in some fast-breaking circumstances, executives may simply not have the time to handle multiple individual interviews. (3) When in-person interviews bring the reporter to your offices, they also add to your concerns, since you'll have to consider everything from grooming and posture to decor.

Editorial board meetings: If you have something significant to say that has broad implications for a community or industry, consider approaching key local newspapers or even major business publications to host an editorial board meeting. The premise of an editorial board meeting is that you will discuss a topic so significant that the news organization will want to take a formal stand on it and announce that stand in an editorial. At such an occasion, you present your ideas for the review and questioning by the paper's "editorial board"—senior editors and editorial page writers. Typically, the reporters who cover your company or industry will also be invited to attend. Although by definition there will be a number of individuals present, because they collectively represent the news outlet as one single entity, you should consider this an individual channel.

- *Advantages:* Editorial board meetings (1) offer potential endorsement by a powerful third party that can help persuade other audiences of your point of view; (2) convince a news organization that it should look at your company, your industry, or your issues in a different light; and (3) may lead to a "trickle-down" effect, positively influencing the perspectives of individual reporters who work for the media outlet.

- *Disadvantages:* This channel (1) requires extensive preparation that includes researching and developing a point of view that goes far beyond the promotion of a single news story, and (2) risks alienating people at the most senior level of a news organization if you don't offer compelling insights.

3. Targeting broad media audiences

Rather than target a single reporter, in some situations you may want to interest a wider group of reporters or media outlets—as described in the following section.

Press conferences: The press conference has a long tradition in media relations. The standard format involves inviting an audience of reporters to hear a prefatory statement and then opening the floor to questions. Press conferences can be large events with a hundred journalists assembling to learn about a major merger or acquisition, or small gatherings of half a dozen trade reporters meeting to hear about a new product. Some are elaborate affairs scheduled weeks in advance; others are impromptu gatherings called in response to breaking news. Despite its long tradition, however, the press conference is a channel that is being used less often today as a means of conveying timely information.

- *Advantages:* (1) Press conferences generate a ready-made package of hard news and camera-ready visuals all happening at one convenient time and place. (2) They validate the importance of the news you're making. Even if only a few reporters show up, the fact that the press conference took place makes your news more "real." (3) They also showcase your executives' leadership in a format that serves more audiences than just the media; employees, major customers, and shareholders can also be invited to attend.

- *Disadvantages:* (1) Press conferences take time to organize, which means the news can be old before the event itself begins. (2) They put senior executives on display for all to see. Unless they are media trained and media savvy, executives may find this public theater beyond their capabilities. (3) Press conferences are also difficult to control: company spokespeople may be at a severe disadvantage when confronted with a barrage of questions from reporters or by adversaries who gate-crash your event and pose challenges from the floor. (4) Finally, press conferences may not be worth the expense if too few reporters show up to make the event worthwhile.

Conference calls and webcasts: One device helping to replace the in-person press conference is the telephone conference call. Reporters are invited to call a prearranged "dial-in" number at a set time. Management begins the call, as they would a press conference, with the news announcement and/or scripted remarks, before turning to questions from callers. A telecommunications service provider moderates the flow of questions. Conference call audio can also be broadcast over the Internet via your company website, a technique called a "webcast."

- *Advantages:* (1) Conference calls and webcasts offer convenience: they can be set up quickly, run from any office with telephone access—or even multiple locations—and eliminate the need for travel. (2) They may also include presentation graphics that listeners can view during the call.

- *Disadvantages:* (1) Conference calls and webcasts highlight poor preparation or a narrow focus. (2) They challenge executives who are uncomfortable responding to questions posed by disembodied voices coming out of the phone. (3) They lose any "bonus" that a dynamic executive might get for live interaction with an audience, since many nonverbal elements are lost over the phone. (4) They may also lead some executives to become too relaxed, bored, or simply careless with the information they release.

Media availabilities: A compromise between a full press conference and time-consuming multiple interviews is called a "media availability" (or "media avail"). You make your spokesperson available for a set ten or fifteen minutes, satisfying the media's need for real-time comment, and then get the busy executive back to business. It can be a valuable way to communicate about a breaking news story.

- *Advantages:* The "media avail" (1) offers a quick interaction in a location of your choice—one that can show off your facility or be convenient for the press; (2) allows you to exert control of the situation, as opposed to "ducking" questions or hiding; (3) simplifies logistics, since it dispenses with many of the trappings of the press conference; (4) seems to be more impromptu, which can translate as less staged and more "real"; (5) meets the needs of the electronic media, which generally prefer having an "actuality"—that is, real people, talking in their own voices and with their own images; and (6) limits the questioning time.

- *Disadvantages:* Yet the "media avail" can (1) seem staged or too rushed, leading the media to feel manipulated, which could be reflected in their coverage; and (2) pose unexpected challenges just like any live event—for example, embarrassing intrusions by onlookers or aggrieved parties can occur.

Press briefings: One way to establish control in an ongoing situation (like a crisis or a labor dispute), where a company is subject to a constant stream of reporters' inquiries, is by providing information to the press at regular intervals via "press briefings." Briefings, if needed, can be scheduled on a daily or weekly basis.

- *Advantages:* Press briefings (1) help you organize your time and maintain control of the flow of information, (2) alleviate some of the difficulty involved with satisfying the media's constant need for details during a continuing crisis situation, and (3) can be combined with updates on your website, where posted information can keep interested media regularly informed.

- *Disadvantages:* These briefings may (1) outpace you, allowing rumors to enter the news flow and receive credence between briefings; or (2) backfire if used inflexibly. (If you absolutely refuse to be available between scheduled briefings, allegations may be reported and not receive rebuttal, or journalists may seek out unreliable or antagonistic sources to make deadlines.)

Social roundtables: Sometimes called a "briefing breakfast" or "roundtable discussion," this channel blends several approaches. Social roundtables bring together a handful of journalists to meet with a senior executive over breakfast or lunch.

- *Advantages:* Social roundtables (1) save time for busy executives by multiplying their efforts, which means executives do not need to repeat the same speeches, anecdotes, and messages time and again; and (2) provide an informal opportunity to convey the intangible positives of personality.

- *Disadvantages:* Social roundtables (1) require that several journalists be willing and able to commit time, at your convenience, for an occasion that may not be unusually interesting or immediately newsworthy, which means they are difficult to organize; and (2) hinder questioning, since journalists may not be willing to ask really insightful questions lest someone else beat them on the story that might result.

Publicity stunts: Getting attention for your story can be a challenge—particularly if you're talking about publicity for your product or service. But going back to the earliest days of PR, attracting attention with a creative gambit has been an important tool of the trade. Particularly in the "dog days" of August or other slack periods, events that offer news cameras a chance to record "The World's

Biggest Bowl of Pasta" or a coast-to-coast linking of "Hands Across America," can also provide a platform for an official announcement. (The giant pasta bowl was a platform for Nintendo's launch of a video game; "Hands Across America" publicized a fund-raising effort to fight hunger and homelessness.)

Today, activist groups, often short on the cash needed for paid advertising, have mastered the art of creating highly visual events to demonstrate their points and grab headlines and airtime. But while activist groups rarely receive criticism for such staged events, companies and industry groups are often censured for them. Some people trip up on the shadowy line separating publicity from misrepresentation.

- *Advantages:* These events (1) leverage the media's insatiable demand for something to report, especially during slow news periods; and (2) leave a lasting, visual impression that helps break through the haze of similar-sounding announcements.

- *Disadvantages:* Yet, they (1) risk the ire of the media and the public if the special event is a front for a hidden commercial interest; (2) can cost more than the benefits are worth when the stunt involves access to public property, staging, and so on; and (3) overshadow the message if the event is inherently more interesting than what it promotes.

Media advisories: Any time you are contemplating a public media event—such as a press conference, conference call, or media availability—you need to alert reporters in advance and get them to block time. Media advisories are the notices you use to accomplish that objective. The art of the advisory is to provide enough information to entice the press to make an appearance or place a call, but not enough to render your event itself superfluous.

- *Advantage:* Media advisories are an all-purpose attention getter, useful whether you're staging a publicity stunt or a serious press conference.

- *Disadvantage:* They may inadvertently convey too much of the story, in which case reporters will simply file their reports from the advisory and not bother to read the release or attend the press event the advisory announces.

Press kits: Whether contained in a plain folder or a fancy box, a press kit is a collection of documents, supplemented with print-ready graphics and/or photographs, that usually includes the "lead" press release announcing the news of the day, a background sheet of key facts about the organization, and bios of relevant/important executives. Supplements could easily include a position paper on a topic, reprints of news articles about the company, and other recent press releases.

- *Advantages:* (1) Press kits provide a reference source that is convenient and easy to duplicate and store. (2) They can be easily adapted for different purposes, such as educating reporters who are just starting to learn about your organization, ensuring that everyone attending a press event has background details, or serving as an informative "leave-behind" for an interview.

- *Disadvantage:* They can become a distraction if excessive attention and resources are devoted to their care and feeding. Don't let the process of maintaining the press kit overwhelm the message content it should serve.

"B-roll" and video news releases: Both of these channels provide television news outlets with the "visuals" they need to do their reports. "B-roll" packages are videos with unnarrated images of your operation at its best—such as employees at work, processes in action, and the company logo on a sign outside you newest facility.

In contrast with B-roll packages, video news releases (VNRs) have sound and provide a distinct narrative. They look like news footage, but they are produced by a company that is trying to frame a topic and control its content. As the name implies, VNRs are delivered to media outlets, typically by satellite, in the hope that some or all of the package will be picked up as a bona fide news story.

- *Advantages:* (1) These releases let you compile the most positive image possible of the organization. (2) They provide a resource you keep on file, ready to send as needed to new media contacts. (3) They may also convince a news organization not to send an expensive video crew to your plant or office, where in addition to a static shot of your logo, they might also find employees offering unguarded comments.

- *Disadvantages:* (1) These releases cost money: well-produced VNRs are not cheap. Smaller organizations will want to carefully study the costs versus the anticipated benefits before making a commitment to produce one. (2) In addition, after distribution, they require you to cede direct control over your footage. Naively shot scenes of seemingly happy employees or smiling executives may be juxtaposed with disaster footage for visual effect. (3) Finally, they quickly become outdated. A change in executive leadership may not be reflected in what the media have on hand.

Company websites: Company websites are frequently the first place reporters go to start developing the background for a story or to begin researching a company or an issue. Making your site easy for reporters to access and search is an effective way to communicate your important messages. Although websites serve a wide range of audiences, you can create a direct channel to reach the media by establishing a "News" or "Press" section on the site, something that many call a "newsroom." This section would typically contain postings of press releases, fact sheets, and other reference material. Websites can also be used with conference calls to broadcast a webcast of the call. They can provide real-time access to visual materials like a PowerPoint presentation during the call.

- *Advantages:* (1) A web-based media newsroom makes information sharing easier for the user, and for you. A good website becomes a first stop, a resource that enables reporters to ask more relevant questions when they do have you or an executive on the phone. (2) It saves money on faxing, mailing, printing, and storing materials.

- *Disadvantages:* (1) These sites need to be constantly updated by someone competent who also considers the task an important and continuing responsibility. (2) They can annoy users if they promise useful information but fail to deliver it.

Corporate advertising: Corporate advertising is the paid use of media to support a company's position and image (as opposed to conventional advertising that promotes products or services). Usually a full-page printed statement, such ads are frequently couched as "An Open Letter to" in which the intended recipient is one or another stakeholder group. Corporate advertising allows you to get your message across without any media filter. It is often employed during crises to communicate the company's position to all interested parties.

- *Advantages:* (1) Corporate advertising can be a seamless part of an overall media or image campaign. (2) Ads can be sequenced, with the messages extended and expanded to make the company's case, maximizing their impact. (3) In some cases, the advertisements can become a story in their own right, with journalists reporting on the ads and your strategy for placing them.

- *Disadvantages:* (1) Corporate advertising can backfire if ads come across as a smokescreen to divert attention from the "real" story or as the tactic of a deep-pocketed corporation using its financial clout to swamp the voices of opponents. (2) If poorly conceived or designed, ads become symbols of naiveté rather than sophistication.

Third-party support: This channel requires that you identify third parties who share your views on industry or organizational concerns. Sometimes these parties are willing to provide their "unbiased" or at least "expert" perspective when you direct the media to them for comment. Third-party support could come from financial experts, geologists, environmental remediation specialists, or biologists.

- *Advantage:* Third parties can contribute valuable details and guidance for media audiences in responding appropriately to difficult situations.
- *Disadvantage:* If third-party "unbiased experts" turn out to lack credibility or are found to be secretly on your payroll, expect an avalanche of criticism and subsequent investigation from the media and government.

Chapter Summary: CHANNELS TO THE MEDIA		
Channel	**Individually or broadly targeted?**	**Comments**
Press releases	Can be either	Most versatile channel: the common denominator for media outreach.
Pitch letters	Individually targeted to reach a specific media outlet	More personal than a press release; designed to trigger follow-up.
Social interactions		Can create a framework for ongoing contact with a reporter.
Desk-side chats		Convenient for reporters; you stop by their offices.
One-on-one interviews		Most direct channel; can be phone, office, or studio.
Editorial board meeting		Appropriate when your message is significant.
Press conferences	Broadly targeted to reach multiple media outlets	Can be large or small; require careful planning.
Conference calls and webcasts		Offer convenience, but lack the personal dimension.
Media availabilities		Can control time during a breaking story.
Press briefings		Can be scheduled daily or weekly, depending on media interest.
Social roundtables		Gather reporters to meet with senior executives.
Publicity stunts		May gain coverage during slack news periods.
Media advisories		Entice reporters to attend an event, such as a press conference.
Press kits		A "leave-behind" package with background information.
B-roll and VNRs		Provide broadcast outlets with footage you produced.
Company websites		Allows for multiple postings, including video footage.
Corporate advertising		Gets your message across with out any media filter.
Third-party endorsement		Can provide credible support to your position.

CHAPTER II OUTLINE

I. Developing a newsworthy message
   1. What makes it news?
   2. How can you interest the media?

II. Getting to know your important reporters
   1. Research your targets
   2. Create your press list
   3. Establish relationships with reporters
   4. Establish guidelines for media contact

III. Using your media channels effectively
   1. Creating and distributing press releases
   2. Communicating with individual media outlets
   3. Communicating with broad media audiences

IV. Engaging media professionals
   1. When to employ an agency
   2. How to choose among the pack

CHAPTER II

Cast Your Line: Developing Proactive Media Relations

Y ou may think you have a very compelling news story that reporters should be clamoring to cover. But every day, the two major press release distribution services put out an average of 2,500 press releases. At the same time, there are ongoing developments in your industry, and in the economy in general, that reporters and their news organizations are already interested in covering. Your story is competing in a no-holds-barred battle to command the attention of the media: that is your primary challenge.

Getting the media to pay attention to your news, and to consistently report on your organization in as favorable a manner as possible, is called "media relations." This chapter covers three main elements of media relations: (1) developing messages and stories that the media will consider newsworthy, (2) establishing ongoing relationships with the media targets you want to cover your organization, and (3) employing the channels defined in the previous chapter to carry your messages to those media.

I. DEVELOPING A NEWSWORTHY MESSAGE

Getting the media to pay attention to your stories is a sales and marketing job. You have to start by adopting a selling or "pitching" attitude. Too many business executives believe that "good news stories" are precisely what the media *should* run about their firms. They think it's the media's job to come to them and find out what good news they've got. This belief is simply executive fantasy. Companies are *supposed* to be well run.

In reality, you need to frame your messages and stories so that they will meet journalists' standards for coverage. And you need to take a proactive approach to getting your newsworthy stories in front of the right media.

If you were fishing, you might begin by asking yourself: "Am I trying to catch a whole school with a net or am I hoping to hook one big fish on my line?" With news, you face a similar decision. Your strategy should be based on the nature of your news and your ultimate business objectives. A "net strategy" may be right for launching a consumer product: pushing your news out to the broadest audience in the shortest time. By contrast, a "hook strategy" may work better for a complex story targeted only at your investors. Using the "hook," you could focus on one business reporter at the top local paper who, past experience suggests, interprets the news accurately. Ideally, her report will influence local radio and TV, and maybe even make the Associated Press wire, where it can be picked up by papers and broadcast outlets across the country.

Once you've adopted this strategic mind-set, you can put the channels of media relations—press releases, press conferences, and the like—to work for you.

1. What makes it news?

News is what's new or different. To meet the test of newsworthiness, your story must show how your company, product, or latest development is differentiated from everything else happening in the marketplace. What's new will register on a reporter's radar. Framing the company message in a creative or expressive manner can also set it apart from the ordinary and make it rise above the "noise."

Before you can begin, you need to genuinely understand what is unique about your story. You need to be familiar with current developments in your industry and with what your competitors are doing and saying. Business as usual is not "news"—innovation, change, and "The Next Big Thing"—these are the hallmarks of what is newsworthy.

Writing a Media Relations Plan helps to clarify if something is newsworthy. Whether you're planning the biggest new-product launch in the history of your industry or just announcing an executive appointment, you should have a plan that: (1) defines your business objectives, (2) captures your differentiating messages, (3) outlines your strategy, (4) summarizes the tactics you'll employ, and (5) lists your media targets. The Media Relations Plan helps you define just what is newsworthy about your story. It also highlights where you'll need additional support, enables you to chart a course to get that story to the media, and gives you a basis for evaluating your success.

2. How can you interest the media?

The best way to engage the media is to offer new insights: tell them something they don't already know. You might also try to link your story to larger trends or issues that the press is already following. Either way, you will be helping the media to do their job, which involves not merely discovering what is new, but also uncovering new perspectives on what is important.

Know how their job has changed.   In today's electronic environment, news announcements and media coverage are transmitted instantly and circulated on newswires and the Internet, without waiting for daily papers or the six o'clock news. This environment has forced a fundamental change for journalists. According to Claudia Deutsch, business reporter for the *New York Times,* "Newspaper reporters really haven't been able to break news [i.e., be the first to report a story] since television. But now even the television reporters can't break news. Because of the Internet, reporters need not just report the news, they now have to interpret it and take it further."

Be able to go beyond the facts.   This evolution highlights the importance of providing reporters with insight and perspective rather than just basic facts that get old fast. Reporters come to rely on those who take the time to provide that kind of context, who explain their company's position on a critical issue, and above all, who appreciate the reporters' needs and play it straight with them.

Adapt to the situation.   Depending on your targets, you can use various channels (described on pages 12–23) to reach out with information that would pique media interest in your story. Your approach can range from the cerebral to the emotional—from thoughtful pitch letters to creative stunts. But keep in mind that however you approach your initial foray, you'll need to back it up with substance.

II. GETTING TO KNOW YOUR REPORTERS

Once you are confident that you know how to develop a story, you need to target the right reporters with your media marketing efforts. Ultimately, you want to establish open avenues of communication with them.

You can accomplish this task by: (1) researching the relevance of particular media outlets to your objectives, (2) creating a "press list" of individual journalists at those relevant media outlets, (3) developing productive working relationships with key reporters and editors from your list, and (4) instituting policies and processes to facilitate and direct contacts between your organization and the media.

1. Research your targets.

Proactive media relations are built on a foundation of research and analysis that helps you identify first the news organizations that you want to approach with your stories and then the individual reporters and editors you will need to contact. The most basic research you can do to evaluate the media is to read publications and watch and listen to electronic media.

Recognize the key differentiators.   Key things to keep in mind in discerning the differences between various media are:

- *Audience:* Most media outlets have fairly well-defined audience profiles. Who are they writing or broadcasting for? Consumers who want to know if a product is safe? Or business people concerned about the economic impact that new regulations will have on sales?

- *Beat:* Understand each media outlet's "beat," the specialty or territory it covers. In covering the launch of an innovative new DVD player, technology trade publications will want to cover what's inside the box, consumer electronics reviews want to know how it's better for viewers, and marketing trades will want to know the details and cost of the advertising campaign. Within news organizations, individual reporters have their own special beats as well.

- *Geography:* Location can have an important impact on media priorities. For example, although both are in Florida, the *Tampa Tribune*'s business desk doesn't have much interest in a just–launched medical company located in Orlando. Why? Because Tampa readers don't really have an interest in smaller businesses operating outside their market.

- *Deadline:* Knowing when a news organization needs information can affect whether it will find a place for your story. Does the reporter need those details he asked about for a story he's filing this afternoon for tomorrow's daily paper? Or, is she working on a "think piece" for a monthly trade publication and next week will be plenty of time for an answer?

Focus so you can set priorities.   To prioritize your media outreach, you'll need to start with a careful assessment of the identities of your significant stakeholders and understand which media exert the greatest influence on their perceptions.

The relative importance of different kinds of media will also relate to the essential nature of your business. Consider a company that depends on broad consumer sales, a soft drink company perhaps. Mainstream television news (the morning shows and nightly news reports of the major networks) and general news channels (like CNN and FOX) typically assume great importance for this kind of organization. Yet there are many other factors to consider when setting priorities:

- *Determine each media's relevance.* Relevance can shift, depending on changing circumstances or business objectives. When support is needed on issues involving financing or transactions, coverage in a business daily like the *Wall Street Journal* or the *Daily Deal* can speak most directly to audiences in the banking and legal community. Regional variations on the theme abound. For companies dependent on decisions made "inside the Beltway," coverage in the *Washington Post* is critical. Similarly, for those in the entertainment industry, the *Los Angeles Times*, Hollywood's hometown paper, looms large.

- *Recognize the importance of local media.* Local print, radio, and TV can quickly shape the opinion and influence the goodwill of employees. You may inadvertently create problems for yourself if you marginalize local media outlets to curry favor with the national press. For example, if "sources close to the company" leak an important news story to the *Wall Street Journal* to impress investors, this leak may create lingering resentment on Main Street among local media who can only play catch-up the next day. Companies generally have to live longer and more intimately with their local outlets than with the national media.

- *Recognize the importance of trade publications.* More than one communication professional has asked, "Why bother my boss with a trade publication? Can't some manager in marketing handle it?" Marketing managers might well be the best people to handle a particular inquiry from a trade publication—nuts and bolts details are their bread and butter. But don't sell the trades short—industry leadership is an essential building block for corporate and CEO reputation and trades are the door to that world. General business and consumer media reporters, as well as the financial and investment communities, turn to trade publications as a source of information. Building a close relationship with the trade publications in your industry can enhance your organization's visibility and reputation.

- *Recognize the importance of the Internet.* The "Internet" is not a single medium, but a catchall that encompasses everything from company websites and online versions of mainstream media organizations to chat rooms where disgruntled employees can vent about their companies. Realize that members of the news media have ready access to all the varied sources of information and disinformation that the Internet can provide. Therefore, the Internet can become a hydra of unexpected challenges: (1) email can rapidly spread e-rumors that can affect reputation; (2) activists or hackers can create web pages designed to simulate "official" sites; or (3) company bulletin boards can register the thoughts of disgruntled employees, or of speculators who pretend to be employees to deliberately undermine a company's stock price. Managing the multiple communications challenges posed by the Internet goes well beyond the scope of media relations.

Use available research resources. Thanks to increased general interest in the business of the media, an incredible wealth of available information exists about both media organizations and individual members of the press. Among them:

- *Directories:* Detailed descriptions of newspapers; business magazines; trade publications; the news operations of radio, television, and cable networks and stations; and other news outlets are compiled and updated by several tracking services. Their directories, available by subscription, can be found in many research libraries. Online versions are also available. Two of the most used are: (1) *Bacon's Directories* and (2) *The Yellow Book.*

- *Media newsletters:* Professional communicators have their own equivalents of trade publications and newsletters, and for that audience the comings and goings of reporters and editors is news. Two newsletters that regularly track media developments are: (1) *Bulldog Reporter* and (2) *O'Dwyer's PR Newsletter.*

- *Websites devoted to media analysis and commentary:* Perhaps in character with the investigative tradition of the profession, journalism is a highly introspective profession. As a result, websites devoted to media analysis and commentary have emerged, among them those maintained by: (1) Center for Media and Public Affairs (www.mpa.com); and (2) Project for Excellence in Journalism (www.journalism.org).

- *Services that provide background information:* The TJFR Group's *NewsBios* service (www.newsbios.com) is one example of fee-based services that will provide biographies of individual journalists, noting their educational background, career history, and areas of specialization.

- *Public relations agencies and consultants:* Public relations agencies and consultants specialize in outreach to the media, and, as part of their service offering for their clients, prepare detailed briefings on the media outlets and the specific journalists who would be important to a particular client's overall communications strategy and program.

- *Professional organizations:* The Public Relations Society of America (PRSA), the Publicity Club of New York, and similar organizations regularly run "Meet the Media" programs that offer members a chance to attend presentations by journalists and panel discussions of media needs. Local chapters can provide details and meeting calendars.

Follow reporting about the media.   The media themselves have become the subject of extensive news coverage, much of it in specialized publications and programs. Scholarly explorations of journalism will appear in journals like *The Columbia Journalism Review;* more accessible discussions of media trends and issues can be found in programs like National Public Radio's weekly *On the Media.* But as high-profile journalists become celebrities, and the business of news is increasingly treated like any other industry, stories about media topics and media people can regularly be found in the business sections of consumer newspapers and in publications like the *The New Yorker* and *Vanity Fair.* Today, news anchors' contract talks can even make the page six gossip columns of the *New York Post.* Simply paying attention to this steady stream of reportage can rapidly increase your level of media sophistication.

2. Create your press list.

Once you have researched the relevant media, you will be able to create the press list you'll need to contact key media sources and keep abreast of coverage. Here are six tips to help you determine your press list:

1. *Find out who has reported on you previously.* Identify which reporters and media outlets have previously covered your company. Those who have written about you in the past can be presumed to have continued interest.

2. *Identify those who have reported favorably about your company.* It's common sense to make a priority of ensuring that reporters who have been covering your positive news continue to have the access they need to keep doing that in the future.

3. *Identify those who have reported on the competition.* After all, the competition may have a more established PR program and may be reaching out regularly to key reporters.

4. *Use reference works to help you categorize.* Media directories can help identify outlets by geography or subject, and within those categories, reporters by individual beat assignments.

5. *Gather contact data.* Assemble your press list to include: (1) the name of each media outlet, (2) names of individual reporters and editors, and (3) their specific beats, their phone and fax numbers, and their email addresses.

6. *Put together a spreadsheet.* Almost as important as identifying the right individuals is putting the information about them into an easily usable form. You'll best accomplish this task if you maintain your media information as a spreadsheet. Spreadsheets are easy to update and customize for special applications. In an electronic format, they can be used by distribution services for mailings and "blastfax" (mass-distributed faxes applications).

SAMPLE PRESS LIST
FOR A NEW YORK ENTERTAINMENT COMPANY

Wire services: Dow Jones, Reuters, Bloomberg, Associated Press

Dailies: the *New York Times*, the *Daily News*, the *New York Post*, the *Wall Street Journal*, *El Diario*, the *Amsterdam News*, the *Sun*

Weeklies: *The Observer*, *The New Yorker*, *New York*

Trade publications: *Multichannel News*, *Broadcasting and Cable*, *Cable World*, *Advertising Age*, *Media Week*

Business magazines: *Fortune*, *Forbes*, *Businessweek*

Area business: *Crain's New York Business*

Radio: WCBS Newsradio 88, 1010 WINS, Bloomberg 1130

Cable news: CNN, CNBC, FOX News

Local television: WABC TV, WCBS TV, WNBC TV, WOR TV, WFOX, and others

Long as it seems, even this list isn't complete.

Specialized trade publications: Each area of the company's business may have its own specialized trade publications. For example, if it owns movie theaters or sports arenas, there are publications devoted to the business of those fields. Specialized talk-radio programs for sports would also find a place on this list.

Suburban newspapers: If it has operations outside the five boroughs that make up New York City, other daily papers would also be important.

Weekly community newspapers: These play a role in shaping opinion about the company—especially in communicating about its local operations. Cable television, transportation, telephone, and utility companies are heavily covered in such publications.

Individual reporters: At each publication, station, and network, there may be five or six individual reporters and/or editors who have an interest in different aspects of the company.

3. Establish relationships with reporters.

Once you have a press list, get to know and understand the reporters who cover your company or industry. Journalists come in all shapes and sizes. Some are old hands with decades of experience. Others are fresh out of school—typically journalism school, or undergraduate programs in communications. Each is an individual whom you had better get to know.

Use a customer focus.   Establishing relationships with the media is partly a marketing exercise. When you sell your company's products or services, you need to build relationships with your customers. In this case, the customer—as skeptical as any other, as given to fads—is a journalist.

Use a marketing approach.   After people in your marketing department use consumer research to identify the demographics they want to target, then they get out and talk to the potential customer to better understand the customer's motivations. You need to do the same thing. Get to know the people on your press list. Learn what their interests are, since you've identified them as important to you.

Introduce yourself.   Work your way down your target list, telephoning to introduce yourself. Suggest that you'd like to drop by the reporter's office for a quick introductory chat. Or offer to do the same over a cup of coffee in their cafeteria, or lunch at a convenient restaurant; the venue isn't important. No matter how long you've been at the job, it's never too late to start improving the relationship with the reporters who cover you.

Keep in touch.   Once you have made the introductions, you need to keep in touch with this audience. Create occasions for interaction. Invite reporters to events that your company sponsors—sports events, concerts, charity bashes, industry luncheons, and awards ceremonies. Invite them to the company holiday party or create a separate reception for the journalists who cover the organization. But keep these kinds of events low-key, nonpitch occasions.

Keep up with reporter turnover.   There is ongoing turnover in the media. Although some main players grow familiar in their roles—like the "old lions" who anchor the three networks' nightly newscasts—the media as a community is an ever-changing cast of players. This year's crop of "J-School" graduates feeds the constant demand for fresh talent and moves into rookie slots at daily papers and trade publications, or assignment desk roles at local television stations. That turnover gives corporate communicators opportunities to develop relationships as they teach the neophytes of the press corps the intricacies of their industries.

Invest in the future.   Laying a solid foundation with the press corps that covers your organization ideally allows you to build trust and goodwill among the reporters with whom you interact. The time and effort you spend on these kinds of media relations are an investment against the time when you need to place a marginal story on a busy news day, or need credibility in a crisis.

Keep building your knowledge base.   Maintain a dialogue with reporters: their perspective can provide you with valuable information about your industry, your competition, and even your company. Here are some questions you might ask reporters:

- Do they belong on your list in the first place?
- What are their opinions of your organization and of the individuals in charge?
- From their perspective, what works in the existing relationship? What could be better?
- What do they think of their peers on your list?
- What do they consider newsworthy?
- Have you got their particulars right—deadlines, beat, etc.?

Don't blow it.   Just remember that credibility is your ultimate product. Should your reputation for credibility ever be damaged, should you be caught in a lie, you'll be a long time repairing the damage.

4. Establish guidelines for media contact.

When the media either responds to you or initiates contact, you'll need organizational guidelines to ensure the effective release of information. To do this, you need to (1) coordinate access and (2) connect with the media at the right level.

Coordinate access to the media to ensure consistency. Media contact, like all communications, is about maintaining and enhancing reputation. Delivering consistent messages helps with this goal. Only by coordinating outreach and contact can you achieve such message consistency: you'll need to know what is being said, to whom, and in what context.

- *Centralize media contact.* Ensure that all media inquiries are routed through a single individual or department. Where a corporate communications function exists, that is the logical place to house media relations. As the single point of routine contact, the media relations coordinator will evaluate media inquiries, set priorities for responding, identify appropriate spokespeople for each request, and conduct follow-up. Restrict everyone in the organization from reaching out to the media without first clearing it through the media coordinator.

- *Communicate procedures internally.* Provide instructions for managers and employees that clearly outline how to refer all media inquiries to the central clearinghouse. For smaller organizations, this task will be relatively easy to accomplish. For larger ones, guidebooks and intranet website posting will be helpful. Keep this information up-to-date and ensure that department heads and support staff understand the need for these policies—and why media relations are important to the organization's success.

- *Keep your strategic purpose in mind.* Every media interaction should be an opportunity to communicate the organization's key messages—as adapted to whatever situation is at hand. To maintain this strategic focus, the media relations coordinator should ensure that anyone speaking with media reinforces those messages in all of the media channels described on pages 12–23.

Connect with the media at the right level. Across the spectrum of possible company contacts, reporters and editors need to feel that your organization is responsive to them and not ignoring or stonewalling them. In the age of the Internet, with chat rooms and discussion sites serving up comments on virtually every organization, there is almost always some outside source that a reporter can quote about you.

Although reporters may start out asking to talk with the CEO, a responsive comment or interesting insight from further down the chain of command is usually more than welcome if it can help complete the story.

The media coordinator must determine which person in the organization can best respond to the question at hand. Not every inquiry demands response by a senior executive or even an official spokesperson. Depending upon the seriousness of the subject, the kind of information needed, the type of media involved, and the reporter asking the question, most responses can be conveyed by the following kinds of respondents:

- *Media relations coordinator/spokesperson:* This person needs sufficient information and authority to act as an official spokesperson on routine matters. With that authority, the communications officer can determine when it is necessary to move up the chain of command to secure more specific information or insights; for example, engaging senior executives if matters of reputation, corporate strategy, and financial performance need to be addressed.

- *Marketing, technical, or line executives:* Trade publications live and breathe for the details of promotional campaigns or a discussion of the technical specifications of a new product offering. Senior marketing executives, salespeople by nature, are often perfect for describing the benefits of a new campaign or product launch. With the kind of training discussed in Chapter III, even the most "gear-headed" of technicians can learn how best to translate personal enthusiasm for a new widget into great "spin" for targeted media.

- *"C-Suite" executives* (corporate leaders whose titles generally start with the letter "C"—i.e., CEO, CFO, CIO, General Counsel): It's become a given that corporate reputation is ultimately embodied in the person of the CEO. For good or ill, the media have come to use the personality of the most senior officer as a proxy or metaphor for the soul of the company. On matters of reputation, financial performance, and corporate strategy, the ultimate spokesperson therefore is the CEO. As part of the process of setting priorities, you will have to work with senior management to keep them accessible when circumstances warrant (as in a crisis), while also setting priorities that enable them to fill this role without distracting from the serious business of running the company. Circumstances will differ for each organization.

Failure to coordinate access and connect with the media at the right level has a real downside. Whenever a story appears that contains the line, "the company was not available for comment," it's almost always a sign of lost opportunity.

III. USING YOUR MEDIA CHANNELS EFFECTIVELY

With your press targets in sight, you need to effectively and efficiently use the channels that you have available to communicate with them. Different channels will be appropriate under different circumstances. This section offers some guidance on how to employ the main types of media channels. More specifically, it addresses (1) creating and distributing press releases, (2) communicating with individual media outlets, and (3) communicating with broad media audiences.

1. Creating and distributing press releases

The press release is sent directly to media and to any other audiences to whom you want to tell your story. Some releases may be nothing more than lightweight efforts to attract some attention for your company's name on an otherwise slow news day. Others can be very serious.

In the case of financial news, the press release takes on the duties of a legal document; it is recognized by government regulators as the instrument of your formal disclosure of investor information. For this reason, senior management, legal, and other counsel should carefully review press releases concerning significant business news before they are distributed. (Financial releases are discussed in Chapter IV.)

Follow these six steps for a good press release:

1. *Make headlines punchy or direct.* Your headline summarizes the news in a few words. It can either state the facts or present the interesting "news hook" you think will capture media interest.

2. *Put the news up front.* You've got to capture the reporter's or editor's attention by the end of the first paragraph. Make them want to read the second paragraph.

3. *Give them a quote.* Quote someone in the organization who is responsible for the development you are announcing. A quote provides perspective and context for the basic facts and can be a platform to communicate key messages to varied stakeholders.

4. *Write so your mother will understand it.* Your release will have a life of its own once it is distributed. Make sure your messages and news are readily understandable by anyone who is likely to come across the release. Avoid jargon.

5. *Put additional data on a fact sheet.* Don't clutter your release, which should be a news story, with every specification of a new product, or pages of facts and figures. If there are that many important details, add a separate fact sheet as a supplement.

6. *Save "boilerplate" detail for the end.* Background facts on the company or organization go at the end of the release, and can help the media round out their stories. If two or more organizations are involved in the news, each gets a paragraph.

What follows is a "mock-up" for a typical press release, showing how and where to implement the six steps cited above.

TEMPLATE FOR A PRESS RELEASE

1. Make headlines punchy or direct.

WRITE THE BEST HEADLINE YOU'D LIKE TO SEE IN TOMORROW'S PAPER

Add a Subhead that Provides a Key Detail or Two

2. Put the news up front.

CITY AND STATE WHERE THE NEWS HAPPENED, ANNOUNCEMENT DATE

Company (include stock "ticker" symbol for public companies), the country's/world's largest/best at whatever you do, today announced in about ten words just what this is all about.

In the beginning of the release describe the benefits this development will have for specific audiences. Using bullet points is often a good idea. Some examples might include:

• More jobs for employees
• Better prices or products for customers
• Environmental benefits for the community
• Improved earnings and a higher share price for stockholders

3. Give them a quote.

The most senior executive possible said, "A pithy two to three sentences that comment on the importance of this announcement in a way that adds a personal dimension to the news." You're writing to persuade the media that the senior executive's quote is both insightful and succinct enough that they will want to run it as part of their story. If your release is going on to two pages, make sure the quote is on page one.

4. Write so your mother will understand it.

Make sure your messages and news are readily understandable by anyone who is likely to come across the release. Some additional supporting details—facts, figures, and so on—can be added to the body of the release. The media do need details, but don't get bogged down with minutiae in the opening paragraphs before you set the context and say why the news is important. Details come later.

5. Put additional data on a fact sheet.

If you have a great many details to report for your trade publications or the financial community, consider adding a separate fact sheet rather than trying to make sentences and paragraphs out of them. For example, for earnings releases—a type of press release intended for financial media—use tables for the income statement and balance sheet details.

6. Save "boilerplate" detail for the end.

Boilerplate should go at the end. This is a paragraph (or paragraphs if two or more companies/organizations are involved in the announcement) that states what the company does, what the principal lines of business are, how many employees it has, where its main operations are, and so on. The boilerplate is repeated at the end of every release you issue, and needs to change only as the business changes.

# # #

(A symbol to let the media know they've reach the end of the release)

Keep your press release concise.   Executives—particularly those with sales backgrounds—frequently believe that it's necessary to get everything they have to say about a new product or other news into the press release announcing it. They forget just how much news is being pumped into the market every day, and how difficult it can be to cut through the clutter. A good press release stands apart from that clutter; it does not contribute to it.

Distribute your release efficiently.   Most companies use one of the paid distribution wires to handle distribution of press releases: *Business Wire* and *PR Newswire* are the biggest and most commonly used. These essential resources maintain their own databases of media contacts and can ensure that a news release gets into most newsrooms in the country—from wire services to the nightly news— virtually simultaneously. They can also include specialized trade publications as part of their distribution service, and get your news directly to the financial community.

Don't neglect to follow up as needed.   Proactive communication requires follow-up to ensure that your press release stands out from the hundreds of others that may cross the recipient's desk. So first, do the obvious: check news reports to see if the item has already been picked up. Some reporters are annoyed by calls asking, "Did you get our release?" But if you believe you should have received a response, it's wise to ensure that the release didn't get lost, or addressed to someone who is out on vacation. Naturally, your standing press list (see page 36) gives you a start.

Time your release effectively.   Once you've decided *how* to distribute your release (how broadly or how targeted an audience you are pitching, whether or not to use a distribution service) the next most important question is *when* to release the news. Is it good news that you want to shout from the rooftops? Or some item of information that you're formally required to disclose, but would prefer not to highlight? The critical point to remember: bad timing can kill your chance for the kind of coverage you want.

- *When during the day:* Releasing your news early in the day gives you the most time in a daily news cycle to work the press, drum up interest, and answer questions. Dumping a release after the stock market has closed on Friday means you're feeding it into the black hole of weekend coverage—with little time for the press to follow up and little space to cover it in the Saturday paper or news broadcasts. (Choosing the late Friday option may also expose you to criticism that you're trying to hide the news, which can become a story in itself.)

- *When during the week:* In general, the earlier in the week you announce a story, the more opportunity you are providing for coverage and media follow-up before it is considered "old news." An exception is Mondays—which can become crowded with announcements that have been held over the weekend. So if you release news on Mondays, you run the risk of getting lost in the pack.

- *When during media cycles:* Find out when your industry's trade publications or newspaper weekly feature sections close. Trades often close by Wednesday of the week in advance of publication. This deadline means that if you release your news on Thursday, your story won't appear in print until ten days later and the news might be considered stale by then.

2. Communicating with individual media outlets

In addition to using press releases, use the following individual communication channels (described on pages 13–16) to build long-term relationships with the media.

Pitch letters and follow-up calls: Because a pitch letter is styled as a "personal" approach to an individual journalist, make doubly certain that you are focused on a reporter who is likely to be interested in the subject. Otherwise your pitch is "junk mail."

Avoid attachments. Opening attachments is another time-consuming step that gets in the way of communicating. Some reporters ignore attachments altogether; therefore, cut-and-paste text into your email instead.

Pitch letters commonly end with a line like—"I'll call shortly to check your interest." You are alerting the journalist to expect you or one of your team to follow the pitch letter with a telephone call. Be warned that there are journalists who will bluntly tell you "Never call me again. If I were interested in your story, I'd have called you." But you won't know that unless you try at least once.

Social conversations: Be careful not to become a victim of your own "success" in establishing a chummy relationship with the press. Reporters have a job to do, which is to dig up news, and there will be times when that job puts the individual reporter in an adversarial relationship with a PR person. Keeping those distinct, and at times divergent, responsibilities in mind can help clarify the boundaries of the professional relationships that develop informally.

Desk-side chats: To make the most of your visit, you will want to write out your key points in advance. This is a sales call, not a social occasion. Bring along a "leave-behind" with background materials for additional review. This document can include the numerical data you've referred to or a chronological list of events for background understanding.

One-on-one interviews: The dynamics are similar whether you're using an interview for proactive media relations, or in response to a reporter's inquiry. (We will discuss how to prepare for such interviews on pages 58–66.)

Editorial board meetings: Remember that editorial board meetings are reserved for topics that are worthy of an editorial, subjects significant enough that the publication will want to take a formal stand on them. Don't just show up prepared to chat. You'll be expected to make a formal presentation on the subject you've identified. Keep in mind that you are addressing the publication's most senior editors; include C-suite or other highly ranked executives in your delegation. As with any presentation, come armed with a "leave-behind," a summary of your presentation that your audience can keep for later reference.

3. Communicating with broad media audiences

Contacting an array of media outlets at once has many advantages, but to use these channels (as defined on pages 17–24) effectively, you must pay careful attention to preparation and logistics.

Press conferences: Think of your press conference as communications theater. For example, in a merger, you can place both CEOs on the stage to show unity as their organizations combine. As another example, by holding a press conference at your facility, you can feature a large audience of supportive employees whose continued employment will be viewed as vital to the local community.

Plan press conferences carefully. Even minor problems can distract from your messages, annoy your executives, and if truly bad—your new product doesn't work on stage or an embarrassing picture appears in the computer presentation—the problems become the story. To avoid problems, consider your strategic vision, the cast, the invitation, and the logistics.

- *Strategic vision:* Each element of the press conference should support the overarching message of the event. You need to have clear idea about what that message is—and how each element serves it. For example, if the physical image of your work facility contributes to the message you hope to make, then hold the press conference there. If it would be a distraction, find another site.

- *Cast:* The players should be senior management or those responsible for the subject of the announcement. However, there's a vital prerequisite: you must be confident that you can place your cast in front of an audience that may include hostile questioners. If you can't be certain they'll perform well, then don't incur the time, expense, and distraction of a press conference.

- *Invitation:* Alert the media by putting out an "media advisory" (effectively a mini–press release, as described on page 20) that gives the time and location, and some sense of what will be discussed. For some occasions that are more events than news affairs, you may consider using fancier printed cards and even creative gimmicks to invite the media.

- *Logistics:* Attention to the following details will make or break your press event: (1) *The venue* must be able to handle the crowd, provide access and egress—perhaps for television news crews who are bringing in equipment with trucks—and be convenient for the media.

(2) *Technical requirements* must be considered, including proper lighting, sound equipment, and all the other audio/visual equipment you'll need: check that there will be enough power, parking, and phone lines for both you and the press. (3) *Signage* needs attention: be sure your logo will be visible in photos and on television so the visual impact of the event can register in as many ways as possible. (4) *Speaker and media placement* must be determined: Where will your presenting team be? On a stage? With or without a podium or chairs? Will the press sit apart from others who might attend? Is there an area set aside at the back of the room for television cameras and crews?

Conference calls and webcasts: Technical capabilities and reliability vary among the different service providers who arrange conference calls. You can select a provider by listening to calls of your peers and reviewing their web archives to determine efforts you consider appropriate for your needs. Or you can ask your company's webmaster for recommendations—after all, that's the person who will need to interface with the service provider, and you should be sure they are compatible.

Arrange to have a recording of the conference call available for later replay. The recorded audio provides another channel to which you can direct later callers. The call and accompanying graphic materials can also be archived on your company website.

The current standard for financial relations is to use conference calls to provide follow-up for financial stakeholders, both analysts and investors, after a company announces important financial news. Such calls are discussed in detail on page 83.

Media availabilities: Like the press conference, the "availability" offers some communication theater. After all, management is taking time out from the important business that is the subject of the news, because of their commitment to communications and recognition of the media's role. During the availability, someone will have to take a few questions, but the premise—that available time is short—lets you limit questions and move forward quickly with the event.

In certain circumstances, you might even consider offering the availability via telephone, setting it up as a conference call. Print and radio reporters can get all they need in this fashion; even television outlets can get fresh audio that they can marry to file footage, photos, or other on-screen graphics.

Press briefings: Press briefings should be tied to the news cycles of the media that are important to you, and to the anticipated development of new information in your situation. Briefings can be either oral, where a spokesperson updates the media, or written, by handing out press announcements conveying new developments. The format can be in-person or via conference call.

Social roundtables: You'll need to hang these occasions on some sort of news "peg." In other words, frame them as opportunities to provide perspective on a current event or market condition, or perhaps as updates on plans or projects that have been previously announced.

Publicity stunts: Study the techniques of Edward Bernays, who is often called "The Father of PR." As detailed by the Public Relations Society of America on its website (www.prsa.org), Bernays staged compelling events that drew national attention and created a news platform for the underlying stories of his clients. A famous effort was the 1929 "Torches of Freedom" parade in which women marched up Fifth Avenue smoking cigarettes as symbols of equality—boosting the sales of Bernays' client, American Tobacco. Critics called his events "cheap publicity stunts," but Bernays' triumphs married publicity and strategy—like his promotion of the NAACP's 1920 regional conference in Atlanta that proved a turning point in U.S. race relations.

 The media are always seeking visuals that help enliven their pages or screens. To the extent that your event generates good "visuals," you enhance your chances of success.

Media advisories: Whether announcing a press conference, conference call, or publicity event, the advisory should be structured to show that you'll have answers to four of the five "Ws":

- *What?* A teaser line that provokes interest, but doesn't give away the story.
- *Who?* The bait of senior management or perhaps celebrities who can attract a crowd.
- *When?* The difference between an empty room and a bustling event: schedule events when you're likely to receive optimal response.
- *Where?* The place to be: don't assume every reporter is a local—provide directions.

The fifth W, *Why?*, is what you'll be explaining at your event, and you'll need to provide enough enticement to make attendance beneficial to the reporters.

Press kits: Desktop publishing makes it easy to maintain the basic components of a press kit as electronic files, rather than printing and storing large volumes of material that may soon be out-of-date. This flexibility also enables you to customize press kits, dropping in the latest releases you've issued, and updating any archived information as necessary.

B-roll and video news releases: With B-roll, an accompanying "shot list" identifies what's on the tape, as do introductory frames, which separate the individual video segments. This tape is a resource you can keep at the ready—to hand out or ship out as needed. In addition to "bricks and mortar," B-roll can include images of your executives, perhaps at a past press conference or during another form of media availability, which can be used when visual identification of your organization's managers becomes needed.

VNRs can tell any story your company would like—from the release of a new product line or the appointment of a new CEO to a position statement on a controversial issue. They can be extremely useful when a company wants to provide its take on breaking news. For example, in the aftermath of a hurricane in the Caribbean, one hotel chain released a VNR showing that its facilities and environs were not damaged. The visual footage provided a counterpoint to national coverage showing the storm's destruction.

Some television stations will be reluctant to air VNRs; the ethical question of broadcasting company-produced footage is still debated. However, more and more stations have been using them with identification of their source.

Company websites: Organize your latest news releases, major executive speeches, useful background information, and collateral materials like photo and video files in a separate "newsroom" on the company website. Within that newsroom, you can use a more elaborate technique: establish separate pages or sections for key subjects or issues. (These pages can be as simple as the posting of a white paper or as complex as providing opportunities for visitors to leave comments and feedback.) Some sites even offer the media "subscriptions" that provide access to update services for news from the company (and which provide the company with a handy tool to gather up-to-date email addresses for journalists). A "virtual press kit" with text releases and background sheets, plus electronic image files, can be easily posted on the newsroom page.

As noted above, conference call audio and visual material can be archived on the site for later access or as a research aid for the media and other audiences. Where these involve financial press releases and analysts' webcasts/conference calls, these materials are typically found on the investor relations section of the website, which can be easily linked to the newsroom.

Corporate advertising: Issue-oriented corporate ads are frequently couched as "An Open Letter to. . . ," where the presumed recipient is one stakeholder group or another. That primary target audience may be customers to whom you want to communicate directly, government officials to whom you urge readers to write in support of your position, or even a media outlet that you feel has dealt with you unfairly. But few things in the world of corporate advertising come off worse than a full page of anguished type rebutting a list of "inaccuracies" in a press report. When you see corporate advertising that impresses you, make a note of it and find out who executed the campaign, for your future reference.

Third-party support: Two models exist for effective third-party support: (1) keep a file of articles and other instances where business leaders, academics, government officials, or community representatives express opinions that support yours. When you encounter media pursuing that issue as a story, refer journalists to those citations. (2) Reach out to the sympathetic parties, voice encouragement for their efforts, and explore their willingness to provide commentary that you can incorporate into your materials. This approach can be part of a more comprehensive, grassroots effort to inform and educate audiences about your position on a subject.

IV. ENGAGING MEDIA PROFESSIONALS

If the idea of establishing proactive media relations is too daunting to face alone, a public relations firm can offer valuable assistance for your efforts. In good times, outside counsel can provide logistical support to help implement a media plan. In times of crisis, these professionals can offer suggestions based on experience and even supplement the company's staff as it communicates with critical stakeholders.

The next section explains (1) when to seek outside communications counsel and (2) how to choose among the many public relations professionals in the marketplace.

1. When to employ an agency

There are times when even companies with long-established relationships with their media audience find that outside counsel can add real value to their ongoing outreach. Many of those occasions start with the kinds of transitions that are now common in business:

- Launch of a new company or line of business
- Change due to a merger or acquisition
- Product or organizational crises
- New product introductions
- Kick-off of a new marketing or advertising campaign

A common characteristic of each of those circumstances is that the organization would benefit from expanding its media relationships to include new names and faces in the press corps.

Like legal and financial counseling firms, good public relations agencies provide a wide range of services. More specifically, a PR firm can offer:

- Strategic counsel regarding communications principles and tactics
- Insights into particular news organizations and journalists
- Experience in dealing with the media and in using the channels of communication
- Creativity in developing media approaches and campaigns
- Arms and legs to execute the program

2. How to choose among the pack

Any reputable agency—and that covers the vast majority—is as interested as you are in developing a long-term relationship with clients who value their input. Time invested in the selection process to ensure the agency understands your needs and expectations, and that you understand how they think and work, is time well spent.

Five key steps can help you identify the right communications counsel for you: (1) assess your communications needs, (2) appreciate the distinctions among agencies, (3) conduct research to narrow the field and make a short list of candidates, (4) compare among those alternatives, and (5) meet the top prospects.

Assess your needs.   What you are trying to accomplish? Do you need to reach a broad audience of consumer media in the Top 50 markets, or the fewer than a dozen trade press who follow your industry? Are you facing a food contamination crisis or trying to reinvent the stodgy image of an old manufacturing company? Your needs should influence your selection.

Appreciate distinctions among the agencies.   There are three main categories of communications consultancies: (1) global full-service firms with multiple offices and abilities in most disciplines; (2) local or regional firms that make it their mission to know every local politician, journalist, and newsmaker in their slice of the country; and (3) subject area specialists with deep experience in an industry or discipline.

Research to narrow the field.   Talk with other corporate communicators about their experiences with agencies. Review the recommendations of trade organizations like PRSA for choosing a firm. Consult available directories and listings of the industry, including *O'Dwyer's Directory of Public Relations Agencies* and annual rankings by such trade publications as *PR Week* and *The Holmes Report*. Review the websites of firms that interest you.

Compare alternatives.   Once you've narrowed the pool, develop and circulate a "Request for Proposal" (RFP) soliciting responses from a number of agencies. A typical RFP will describe your firm, outline the communications challenge you face, and ask applicants for information about them that will help you make a decision. The agency replies should include material on their history, philosophy, relevant case studies of past work, and staff that would service your business. You should also ask how they would approach the challenges you outlined, either in general outline, or by providing a detailed campaign proposal. An increasing trend is to use a search consultant similar to an executive recruiting specialist to help with the agency selection process.

Meet the top prospects.   However you winnow the pack, you should meet the top prospects in person before awarding the assignment. It's convenient to invite them to your offices, but you'll probably learn more about their culture and capabilities if you take the time to visit them in their office instead. It can be a sign of how much they want your business if senior agency executives join the meeting. But even if the top guns are on board for this session, don't settle for meeting with them and a new business team that you'll never see again. You want to know who is going to be working on your account, and you want the chance to judge the chemistry you'll have with that team.

Chapter Summary: PROACTIVE MEDIA RELATIONS	
Tasks	**Reminders**
Know what's newsworthy	• Write a media plan. • Understand the roles and the challenges of various media outlets and reporters.
Get to know your reporters	• Create a press list based on extensive research. • Phone and/or visit the reporters on your list. • Establish company guidelines for media contact.
Use a range of channels effectively	• Create well-crafted press releases. • Target individual reporters or individual media outlets using such channels as desk-side chats, pitch letters, or editorial board meetings. • Achieve broader media outreach with channels such as media avails, conference calls, and website "newsrooms." Use media advisories to invite the press.
Engage media professionals as needed	• Assess your needs. • Do your homework to identify possible firms. • Send an RFP once you've narrowed the field.

CHAPTER III OUTLINE

I. Preparing for media interviews
   1. Analyze different interview venues
   2. Learn how to develop your message
   3. Anticipate trick questions

II. Executing the interview
   1. Take control of the interview
   2. Remember your nonverbal communication
   3. Stay focused on your message

CHAPTER III

Caught on the Hook: Responding to Media Calls

The previous chapter explained how you can approach the media and interest reporters in your story. This chapter looks at the opposite kind of situation: when reporters come to you in search of information and you respond to their interview request. We will focus on preparation for, and execution of, the "reactive" media interview when a reporter contacts you.

The need for preparation before reacting to these kinds of interviews rests upon a simple but important premise: reporters are professionals trained to ask questions and to lead the discussion in the direction they want it to go. Their training and purpose are focused on getting *you* to contribute to *their* product, to achieve their design.

More than one executive has wondered out loud, "If the deck is stacked, why bother to play the game?" There is one key reason: every interview can be an opportunity to get your story across. If you take the lead, if you learn to play the game, you can shape the message that gets conveyed to your ultimate audience—the readers and listeners you want to reach.

I. PREPARING FOR MEDIA INTERVIEWS

How often have you heard the subject of a media interview complain, "They took what I said out of context!" Preparation is a way to make sure that what you say and do in an interview helps build the context *you* want and doesn't support opposing images and points of view.

Even in the most friendly of interviews you only have a limited amount of time to get your story across. Preparation helps you make the most of the opportunity that a media interview provides.

Whether you love the media or hate them; whether you believe you have a good, bad, or indifferent relationship with a particular journalist—you have to approach a media interview with a sense of your own personal mission.

Ask yourself two questions:

- What is my overall objective?
- Which points do I want to get across?

You may face time constraints like a deadline in several hours or travel time to get to an interview location. However, you should strive to link your preparation to the news outlet, to the type of interview, and even to the personality and style of the journalist. If time permits, review past examples of this journalist's work, such as videotapes or news clips. Look for trends, such as a predominant interviewing style, recurring topics or interests, or a standard approach, and determine how your messages best relate to them. Also consider the ways different media venues will affect the nature of the prospective interview.

1. Analyze different interview venues.

Your ability to anticipate what's coming, to be comfortable with the experience, and to stay in control of an interview requires an appreciation of the different dynamics that each venue places on its interviews.

Print: Print has the most flexibility. You might be interviewed in person—at your office, or in some other location associated with your business or organization. Most commonly these days, print interviews take place over the phone, giving you the greatest opportunity to control the time, pacing, and length of the session. Telephone interviews also put you in the best position to benefit from the discrete advice of your media advisor, who can "broker" the logistics for the call, listen to the conversation, and slip you advice and reminders either with a quick paper note or an "instant message" on your computer monitor. Just don't be lulled into a false sense of security or complacency with a comfortable interview session in a familiar locale.

Television: Television venues can be varied. The journalist's own studio is one possibility, where hot lights, the formal situation, and the possible celebrity of the interviewer can make it hard for an untrained subject to concentrate on messaging goals.

High drama comes from the TV "ambush," where the journalist, cameraperson in tow, pops out of the bushes or shows up on your doorstep. Long associated with local news stories about cheating auto mechanics, even the television business networks have caught on to the cinematic possibilities of their medium, pursuing Wall Street analysts they've ambushed on the steps of expensive Fifth Avenue cooperative apartments.

Television needs images; that's the business it's in, and you need to think visually when assessing how a particular television opportunity will work for you or against you. For example, effective preparation involves considering the backdrop of the interview. If the local TV station wants to come to your site, you might think about that slick new sign with the company logo on it, outside your building: it could offer a great backdrop for a "stand-up" interview and could help communicate brand identity. But what else will be in the frame? Or audible to the microphones? Happy employees on their way into the facility? Or unkempt grass and dusty vehicles in the parking lot?

Radio: Though greatly reduced in importance as a news medium, radio still provides a tremendous amount of information to key audiences. On the morning you've announced a merger, your employees may well be listening to local news radio during their drive to work. Making yourself available for a quick radio interview—one that stresses the deal's benefits for your company and notes your plans to communicate details to the workforce during the day—can be an important step in a total communications package.

For radio, the telephone interview is the most common vehicle. But distinct from print interviews and more akin to television, your sound bites will carry your messages, while any verbal gaffes or stumbles will provide additional "color" to the interview.

2. Learn how to develop your message.

Since interviews by definition involve someone other than you, to practice for them you will need another person to role-play the reporter. Many companies will engage a professional media trainer to help do this. However, with the help of a colleague, you can train yourself. And if you use commonly available resources to review your responses, such as videotaping or audiotape recording, you will be able to produce a set of training materials for media interviews.

Be aware of the questioner's trap.   Reporters will use the easiest way available to gather the supporting material they need for the big idea that sits on top of the inverted pyramid of their story. In this scenario, the reporter remains in control of the situation, dictating the direction the interview will take. Typically, this is how the process works:

Question/Answer

Question/Answer

Question/Answer

Question/Answer

And so it continues, until the reporter is out of questions. If the interviewee is lucky, she gets thrown a softball at the end—"Is there anything we haven't covered?"

What you want to do is learn how to break that chain of Q/A, Q/A, Q/A, gain control within the process, and communicate your points on your own terms.

Develop memorable messages.   Above all, you want to develop a story and messages to support it. You will need to distill what you have to communicate into easily understood, memorable components. Try to focus on three primary messages. By limiting them, your chance of conveying the message you want to get across will be increased. Typically, most audiences can absorb and remember no more than three thoughts from any single statement. Sculpting what you have to say to that model is your best guarantee of having your messages remembered.

Remember that "sound bites," those quick few words or phrases, perhaps only seconds long, that capture the attention of the producer or editor, will be used to represent all that you have to say.

Some great sound bites are spontaneous, but your interests will be best served if you've taken the time to prepare your message in a form that's comfortable for you.

Two rhetorical devices can also help you deliver memorable messages. They enable you to reshape the Q/A, Q/A, Q/A model of the interview into a vehicle for communicating your messages. These techniques are "bridging" and "flagging."

Practice bridging.   A bridge is a connecting phrase (usually "and" or "but") that carries you from your short response to a reporter's question to one of your primary messages. The model you want to use here is to follow the question with: Answer, Bridge, Message. By using the connective word or phrase, you build a "bridge" that helps you move your response to the message you want to promote or explain. Here are two examples of how bridging allows the interviewee to shape a message rather merely respond to a question:

> "Our plans for expansion are still being discussed but ("bridge") we're committed to serving the changing needs of our clientele and we've already developed new ways of reaching customers to keep them up-to-date about our products and services—our satellite network keeps a finger on their pulse."

> "Yes, we've notified local authorities about the release of gas from our primary processing site. There has been no history of past events of this kind. But ("bridge") we are reviewing our operator training to see how we can improve it and reviewing the computer program to identify what needs to be changed there."

Practice flagging.   This technique calls attention to your messages within a longer answer. Flagging is an auditory device to impress meaning, a metaphorical alert flag to the listener's ears. Typical flags include phrases like:

- "What's at stake here is. . . "
- "Let me emphasize that. . . "
- "Let's remember that. . . "
- "What's critical here is. . . "
- "If you remember one thing, it is that. . . "

Your words alert the listeners to a critical concept that you want them to retain.

Becoming comfortable with these techniques will enable you to dominate the interview—and make it an opportunity to communicate your point of view, your positions, and your information.

3. Anticipate trick questions.

Journalists won't consider them to be trick questions, but once you answer certain inquiries the wrong way, you will certainly feel as if you've been tricked into saying things you never intended. Skilled journalists know how to pose a type of question that provokes responses suited to their task. Learning what these questions sound like and what they're intended to do will give you an equal footing when the interview takes place.

Know the trick questions.

- *Forced choice:* The journalist poses a closed-ended question that artificially sets up an inflexible equation. For example, "What's your biggest problem right now: your falling stock price or your declining employee morale?" Do not buy into the false choice: define your own take on reality.

- *Hypothetical:* The journalist establishes a false premise and creates a situation which does not exist, although one could envision its possible reality. For example, "If the Department of Justice investigates your company's accounting policies and finds your company guilty of criminal behavior, what would you do to reassure investors in the aftermath?" Stick with what is known rather than what could occur: do not speculate.

- *Loaded:* The journalist employs certain charged words or phrases that carry negative connotations. For example, "Your company is part of an industry that regularly pollutes the environment. . . " Do not repeat the negative language, even if you feel you must deny the accusation. When Richard Nixon claimed, "I am not a crook," the repetition of the negative language highlighted not the denial but the negative association.

- *Empty chair:* The journalist refers to third parties and attributes comments to them that may or may not be verifiable. For example, "Senator Smith stated that your company has engaged in potentially fraudulent lending. . . " Do not get into an argument or discussion with an invisible person. Sidestep the question and bridge to your message.

- *Leading:* The journalist prefaces a question with a statement designed to lead you to a conclusion. For example, "Since your CEO has said he will retire at the end of the year, how will the Board of Directors prevent infighting among division heads looking to be promoted?" Reassert your view of the situation, using a flag, and focus on the key message you want to convey. For example, "We've put into place a succession plan, and what's important to realize here is that the company will meet its financial goals for the next quarter and release its next generation of hand-held PDAs on schedule."

- *Emotional:* The journalist invokes sentiment, often by referring to victims or those who have suffered wrong as a result of some kind of event or action. For example, "What can you say to the mothers of the children who today suffer from leukemia after years of playing atop what is now known to be a toxic waste dump?" Do not respond with anger or skepticism. Also avoid responding with bloodless statistics or distancing jargon. Better to express understanding and bridge to a message that's appropriate for the situation, whether it's noncommittal or apologetic. For example, "We've been contributing to the township's hospice and we're aware of the feelings so many people have about this issue. And let me emphasize that we are committed to working with the federal authorities as they begin the site clean-up."

Practice your responses. Dealing with trick questions is never easy. Practice replying to a range of them—until you're comfortable with the rhetorical techniques for defusing the bombs, sidestepping the traps, and getting back on track with your messages. Here are some suggestions to help you as you work through the process:

- *Videotape or audiotape-record your responses* and then listen to them. Gauge your response for logic and appropriateness of language. Ask yourself how the audience would respond to your statements and whether you truly spoke in a convincing, conversational manner.

- *Try answering in three different ways with the same message.* Strive to answer questions with spontaneity and avoid trying to be "perfect." The message you want to convey can be communicated using different sets of words—don't be trapped into using formulaic and robotic phrasing.

- *Avoid rambling.* Get to the point, make your message clear, avoid sounding garrulous.

- *Don't read from notes.* You need to speak to the interviewer directly and not rely upon written supports.

- *Avoid sounding stilted.* Conversational language works best in broadcast venues and should also be reproduced in print to make you appear personable.

- *Don't be argumentative.* Reporters will always have the last word in one way or another. Arguing with them will win you no points.

- *Avoid jargon.* Realize that certain terminology cannot reasonably be expected to be understood by reporters (or your audience.)
- *Cite examples.* People can better grasp a point if they can visualize it or be reminded of an actual situation you describe.
- *Use figures sparingly.* Don't overload with numbers if they interfere with the message you're trying to make.
- *Remember to use bridging and flagging devices.*

Beware of "off-the-record" questions.   Whatever you say to a reporter will become fair game for later use. Attempts to disarm you or shift perspective by alluding to a supposed "off-the-record" moment should raise alarms. More than one interview subject has been badly burned by this gambit. Conversely, you should not assume that by offering an off-the-record comment, the reporter will honor your request. In certain circumstances, you may have a relationship with a reporter whom you trust and whose track record leads you to believe the best. Be advised, however, that like the dozing cat instantly awake at the sound of a bird's chirp, reporters are creatures of opportunity and need—your "good pal" may not be able to resist the lure of a really great story.

II. EXECUTING THE INTERVIEW

Practice lays the foundation for the successful execution of an interview. And to the surprise of many people, successful execution begins even before the actual interview begins. You'll need to set parameters on the reporter's request for information, and as discussed in the next section, impose your own reasonable frame on the interview: time, place, and length need not be left solely to the reporter's discretion.

You also need to keep in mind the way others perceive your body language and facial expressions. Nonverbal behavior must be taken into account as you meet with the reporter and when you find yourself speaking in a broadcast medium. What you say needs to be complemented by how you look. The guidelines presented in the following segments will help ensure that your preparation is linked to effective performance.

1. Take control of the interview.

Even before an interview begins, you need to assert control over the process. Rather than acting as a passive recipient of media inquiry, be prepared to impose structure on your actions the moment a representative of the media makes contact.

Establish control immediately.

Always ask three questions when a reporter phones:

- What is the reporter's name and news organization?
- What is the deadline—how long can you take before answering questions and still be included in the report?
- What is the background for the report—who else is the reporter talking with?

Assess your immediate options:

- Apologize for the fact that you can't take the call right away—and ask how much time you have to get back to them.
- Suggest that you'll have your communications officer contact them in the meantime to get more details on "how we can help you with your report."

Be courteous, but noncommittal:

- Ask your questions about deadline and context without committing yourself to cooperate, at this point, on an interview.
- Consider whether you want to talk to a reporter you don't know, or whose work or media source you don't know.

If you agree to participate:

- Reschedule the interview on your terms and your time.
- Use the time you've bought to do your due diligence. Find out about the reporter and the news outlet.

Avoid being confrontational.   Your goal should always be to take control of the interview process. This doesn't mean turning it into a confrontational process. Remember that there is a profound distinction between taking control and being confrontational. You are in control of a situation when you remain courteous but noncommittal. Therefore, have at your disposal such phrases as these:

> "I'm sorry I can't take your call right now, but tell me what this is about and what your deadline is, and I'll see if we can't help you with your story."

> "I'm sorry, but out of concern for the privacy of our employees, we don't allow television crews to tape inside our facility. But let me know what your deadline is, and a little more about your report, and I'll see if we can make other arrangements to get you someone on camera."

2. Remember your nonverbal communication.

In addition to what you actually say in response to questions, the nonverbal dimension is a critical component for the potential success of the media interview. Posture, attire, facial expression, and gestures are the primary aspects of nonverbal behavior that play a role during interviews, and knowing the common pitfalls can help you avoid unintended and often embarrassing mistakes. Only when you are safely out of the reporter's—or viewer's—eye can you downplay the importance of this dimension and this will only occur during phone or radio interviews.

Television: Look at and talk to the reporter, not the camera. This advice also applies if you are doing a satellite or "half studio" interview. In these situations, you usually can see the reporter on a screen. If there's only a voice in your ear courtesy of an earphone, then you should look at the camera. Consider how you will appear on the screen:

- *Dress appropriately.* Dress in a way that's true to your personality but that avoids calling attention to attire rather than your message. (Avoid white shirts and blouses because of the glare they generate; ties should be simply designed and not overly patterned.)

- *Appear attentive to the question.* Smile politely, as opposed to frowning, though without seeming to trivialize a serious question or situation. Don't nod as you're being asked a question (such moments of agreement can suggest you agree with the reporter's premise even if you absolutely don't). Don't interrupt the question.

- *Reduce signs of nervousness.* Try to avoid undue blinking, licking your lips, or gazing up to the ceiling before answering. If you tend to perspire, and are in a studio, ask to have the air conditioner turned up. If seated, position yourself so that you lean forward slightly; if seated in a swivel chair, remain stationary and don't play with the chair's mechanism. Minimize the use of hand gestures. Hand gestures are important for presentations but are often distracting on film or tape.

If you are the target of an ambush interview, strive to maintain composure: avoid facial expressions that express anger or exasperation; do not use violent gestures; and never attempt to cover the camera lens with your hand.

Print media: Even though there may be no camera in the room with a print reporter, appearance can't be ignored. Journalists looking to add "color" to their reports may cite details of dress, mannerisms, or decor. The reporter is noticing your moods, actions, environment, even your desk.

For example, one freshly minted communications industry CEO was quite pleased with the first interview he'd granted to a business magazine, certain that he'd made all his major points. But once he read that he'd "fumbled" with a television remote and "nervously rattled a pill bottle" (unmentioned that it was for cold medication) during the session, he changed his mind.

Were those denigrating, unfair, and irrelevant characterizations, or vital details that helped capture the essence of the individual and the tenor of the occasion? From the standpoint of control, that debate is irrelevant: both those colorful bits of business were things that, with training and forethought, need not have happened.

3. Stay focused on your message.

What follows are excerpts from a CNN broadcast news interview of July 11, 2001 concerning pharmaceutical companies' marketing costs. The reporter was Brian Nelson; the spokesperson was Alan Holmer, and the consumer advocate was Ron Pollack. Notice how the spokesperson dealt with the loaded question: without repeating the negative aspersion ("smokescreen,") and without sounding defensive, he responded and bridged to his message.

> *Consumer advocate:* So their excuse about skyrocketing prices of drugs, that it's needed for research and development, frankly, is a smokescreen.
>
> *Reporter:* How could this possibly be?
>
> *Spokesperson:* Well, it can't possibly be. And in fact, the numbers that were presented in the initial presentation are extremely misleading. You talked about marketing expenses and advertising expenses, but then when Ron described it, he said marketing, advertising, and administration. When you throw in all those administrative expenses, including for areas outside of the pharmaceutical industry, you're going to have a number that's going to be much higher than what's really the truth. Here are the facts. . .

In the next sequence, the reporter asks a hypothetical question and then interrupts when he doesn't get the answer he wants. Again, the spokesperson does not buy into the hypothetical question and instead, bridges to his message:

> *Reporter:* Is there a case to be made that if there wasn't as much money spent on marketing, the price of pharmaceuticals in this country and around the world would drop?
>
> *Spokesperson:* I really don't think so. Here's the key factor when you talk about marketing and advertising. We have a huge problem in this country with respect to undertreatment and underdiagnosis of disease. If you call the American Diabetes Association, they'll tell you that there are 6 million Americans who have diabetes and who don't know it.
>
> If I could get back to the comment made on CEO compensation. Compensation for CEOs in the pharmaceutical industry is really no different than compensation for CEOs in virtually every other industry in America. As a society, we should want the pharmaceutical companies to be able to attract the best and the brightest, because these are the individuals that are leading the effort to discover and develop new medicines.

Reporter: Can I interrupt here? Yours is an industry upon which millions of people rely for their health, well-being, and sometimes their lives, so this is a different industry than many others. Is there not a case to be made that maybe there's too much money being spent on executive salaries and marketing that could be poured back into reducing the price?

Spokesperson: But again, you want these companies to be led by individuals. You want them to be able to attract the best and brightest, because if you have life-threatening disease the first question you're going to ask your doctor is, "Do you have medicine for that?" You want to make sure that you have the best and the brightest and the most talented individuals to lead these companies that are discovering new medicines for cancer. We've got over 400 medicines in development for cancer, over 100 each for AIDS, heart disease, and stroke.

As the time runs out, the interviewee makes sure to have the last word, concluding with his key message:

Reporter: Last word from you.

Spokesperson: Just one final sentence.

Reporter: OK.

Spokesperson: Profits lead to investment; investment leads to research and development; research and development leads to new cures and treatments—and that's what this is all about.

The final sentence sums up the basic message and concisely conveys it to the listening audience in understandable, jargon-free language.

Chapter Summary: RESPONDING TO MEDIA CALLS		
Phase of interview	**Key tips**	**Reminders**
Preparation	Consider the venue	• Print offers great flexibility since the interview can be done by phone. • TV needs images so think visually.
	Develop your messages	• Distill messages into three memorable points. • Use bridging and flagging to escape the Q/A,Q/A,Q/A trap.
	Anticipate the questions	• Learn how to handle "trick" questions. • Use audio and/or video to rehearse and check your responses.
Execution	Take control of the interview	• Ask the reporter questions before you begin and assess your options. • Be courteous.
	Be aware of nonverbal messages	• For TV, dress appropriately. • Eliminate nonverbal communication that detracts from your message.
	Stay focused	• Keep your objective in mind. • Deliver *your* message whenever you can throughout the interview.

CHAPTER IV OUTLINE

I. Routine financial information
   1. Understanding key financial terms
   2. Reporting quarterly earnings
   3. Reporting material developments
   4. Announcing executive changes

II. Transformational events
   1. Announcing mergers and acquisitions
   2. Announcing restructurings
   3. Disclosing malfeasance

CHAPTER IV

Count the Catch: Dealing with the Financial Media

Dealing with financial media follows the same general principles as dealing with other media. However, it also requires an understanding of their particular dynamics.

- *Who are they?* "Financial media" is a loosely defined term. On one level, it includes every reporter and editor at publications like the *Wall Street Journal, Investor's Business Daily,* and *The Daily Deal*, as well as the staffs of business television programs and networks. But "financial media" also includes the "business" reporters at local daily papers—all of whom might also be covering city hall and museum openings. Between those extremes lies a lot of territory. What that means is that you must be prepared to deal with a wide range of business expertise and financial acumen on the part of journalists who consider themselves "financial media."

- *What do they report?* However defined, at heart, all financial media are driven by one overriding concern: to cover news that will affect the stock markets, either en masse or one stock at a time. The primary audience served by the financial media is investors. And the information needs of all investors—from the largest institutional investors to individuals with a hundred shares in a 401k plan—reduce to a single question: what is going to happen to the value of my stock portfolio?

- *What companies do they report on?* The financial media concentrate their efforts on publicly traded enterprises—those with shares listed on one of the major exchanges or that trade "over the counter." The more widely held the company, the larger its market capitalization, the more important a subject it becomes for the financial press. Consequently, financial media typically have little or no interest in privately held or family owned companies whose investor base is miniscule. An exception is when, as a class, such companies influence overall economic trends or the performance of publicly held companies.

Two general tips to keep in mind when creating and releasing financial announcements are:

- *Coordinate carefully with your organization's fiscal and legal executives.* Serious consequences can stem from challenges to the accuracy and adequacy of a company's financial reporting. And because the regulations governing these areas are undergoing dramatic revision, financial communication today is in transition.

- *Consult two informative websites,* as well as legal counsel for authoritative legal opinions. The U.S. Securities and Exchange Commission (SEC) maintains a comprehensive site on the subject (www.sec.gov) and the National Investor Relations Institute (NIRI), the authoritative professional association of corporate officers and investor relations consultants, also provides valuable guidance (www.niri.org).

This chapter provides an overview of both kinds of financial reporting: (1) routine or required measures of financial performance and governance and (2) transformational events that move the market.

I. ROUTINE FINANCIAL INFORMATION

To appreciate the intricacies of dealing with financial media and communicating financial information, you need to understand the dynamics of a related field called investor relations or "IR." This function handles a company's direct contact with the investment community. Joseph Fitzgerald, head of investor relations at MGM and one of the best practitioners in the business, summed up the role of IR by saying, "Investor relations is the art of managing investor expectations."

Because IR is heavily involved in communicating about financial and accounting issues to an audience that deals largely in numbers, many companies place IR within their finance or treasury operations. However, with a growing appreciation of the important role IR plays in managing overall corporate reputation, some companies position IR within their corporate communication departments. Wherever it is housed, in most organizations IR assumes responsibility for announcing financial news. A common division of labor is that IR takes the lead on preparing financial communications. For inquiries, investors are generally advised to call the IR contacts and media are directed to the PR team.

This section covers routine financial information: (1) understanding key terms, (2) reporting quarterly earnings, (3) reporting material developments, and (4) announcing executive changes.

I. Understanding key financial terms

To conduct financial communications effectively, you first need to understand the following key terms.

Wall Street ("sell side") analysts: One set of important analysts are the "Wall Street analysts," the experts at major brokerage houses who track publicly traded companies, recommend investment options to the firm's clients, and help investors pick stocks that will rise in value. Because they work for firms that trade or "sell" stocks, these analysts are known as the "sell side" analysts. Sell siders' recommendations are published by their brokerage employers, who are looking to attract trading clients. As a result, the analysts most quoted by the press are sell side analysts.

"Buy side" analysts: Another set of analysts in the financial markets are the "buy side" analysts who work at the large financial institutions that actually invest in or buy stocks—insurance companies, pension funds, mutual funds, and so on. The "buy siders" conduct their own research, which may be influenced by the opinions of their sell side counterparts. The buy side analysts are circumspect with their investment opinions, which are considered proprietary to their employers.

Earnings estimates: Expectations, at least those of Wall Street, are expressed continuously in the form of "analysts' earnings estimates." Obviously, investors want to buy stocks that will rise in price or outperform the market and dump those that are stagnant or will underperform. The sell side analysts' earnings estimates—projections of how much money companies will earn in a fiscal quarter or a full year—are key projections of corporate health. They are also the statistical expression of each analyst's investment opinion. Will the company earn more or less in a given quarter than it did the year before or the quarter before? Is the company growing or foundering? It's all in the estimate.

Consensus estimates: Analysts' earnings estimates form the basis for "The Street's" opinions about what a stock will be worth in the future. Movements up or down in these estimates of a company's anticipated future earnings influence the price investors are willing to pay today for the stock. And when a company publishes an earnings release, the financial media are the ones who report whether the earnings met, exceeded, or fell short of the "consensus estimate"—an average of the individual estimates made by various analysts.

Whisper numbers: The past several years have seen a wave of controversy over the reporting of earnings and the relationships between companies and the supposedly independent financial analysts who cover them. During the high-tech bubble of the early 2000s, companies routinely "outperformed" Wall Street's estimates and glowing media reports on that stellar performance filled the financial pages. At the same time, there were suggestions of "whisper numbers"—more accurate estimates that were available to those "in the know"—which more savvy reporters began to comment on.

By 2002, following the crash of dot.com companies and the accounting scandals of Enron, Worldcom, and other former high-flying energy and telecommunications companies, questionable financial reporting practices led to a crisis in confidence for corporate America. Two primary allegations were that: (1) financial sleight-of-hand had been used to report inflated earnings and justify higher share prices; and (2) many research analysts, motivated by the drive to increase investment banking business for their firms, maintained unrealistically bullish public earnings estimates and recommendations for companies they followed.

Disclosure: Even before these scandals broke, various efforts had begun to protect investors through reforms of financial reporting and investment research. These efforts focused on creating a level playing field—ensuring wide dissemination or "disclosure" of financial information to investors. By 2002, two key developments had come together to affect the way companies announce financial data to investors and the press: (1) the SEC's "Regulation Fair Disclosure" and (2) a new focus on making sure that earnings numbers conform with "GAAP accounting," accounting based on Generally Accepted Accounting Principles as promulgated by the Financial Accounting Standards Board, rather than more subjective, and rosy, "pro forma" earnings numbers.

Reg FD: Regulation Fair Disclosure has been nicknamed "Reg FD." The principle behind the rule, indeed, the principle that should guide all financial media relations, is to disclose important corporate information in a timely fashion to as broad an audience as possible. That way everyone, or every investor, has simultaneous access to the news and can act on it, without being beaten to the punch by other investors who benefit from earlier information.

Selective disclosure: The intent of Reg FD is to prevent what is known as "selective disclosure"—which occurs when material information is made available or "disclosed" to a select few. Those few would be able to act on the information to their benefit, anticipating a move in a company's share price, and buying or selling stock before the material news reaches other investors.

Media "carve-out":   The SEC recognized the special role of the media when it created Reg FD and specifically exempted providing information to journalists from the definition of selective disclosure. The rule states, "Regulation FD will not apply to a variety of legitimate, ordinary-course business communications or to disclosures to the media." This policy has been called the "media carve-out" and NIRI has commented that: "In making this exception, the SEC sees the role of the media as disseminators of information whereas those covered by the rule are those who are likely to trade on material, non-public information or use it for trading purposes."

Practically speaking, the media carve-out gives companies some flexibility in speaking with journalists in advance of the broader release of financial news, as we will discuss in the section on merger and acquisition announcements, pages 87–88.

2. Reporting quarterly earnings

Every three months, public companies have to issue a report card on their progress—their quarterly financial statement. This statement, known as a "10-Q," must be filed with the SEC within 45 days of the close of the financial reporting period—a timeframe the SEC is thinking about shortening. It's a benchmark for comparison with the Street's "consensus" estimates.

Before the filing itself, companies announce their results in an "earnings release." This release is generally issued two to three weeks following the close of the quarter. Financial markets closely follow the earnings release—as do the financial media who see the investing public as their audience.

There are three key elements in reporting earnings to the financial media: (1) write the earnings release, (2) time the announcement, and (3) provide further elaboration on the results.

Writing the earnings release: The styles of earnings releases vary widely among organizations—from terse recounting of bare-bones profit and sales figures for the quarter and year-to-date periods, to more elaborate communiqués that explore, in detail, the quarter's developments for each line of business. Whatever the style, earnings releases provide a platform to highlight the company's strategic messages and show how this quarter's performance relates to long-term objectives.

At a minimum, the earnings release should provide:

- Total revenues and net income (or loss) for the quarter and for the year-to-date period
- Percentage comparison of those numbers with the comparable year-earlier numbers
- Earnings-per-share (EPS) for the reporting periods
- Some explanation of the business dynamics that affected performance
- An income statement that shows how the earnings were calculated
- A quote from the CEO or other senior management, commenting on the quarter's performance and relating it to the company's overall business strategy and objectives

Many companies find it useful to add other numbers that are used in their industry sector to evaluate the relative performance of companies. Examples include:

- Cash flow or earnings before income taxes, depreciation and amortization (EBITA)
- Unit sales volumes
- Order backlog

The NIRI has issued new guidelines to help companies prepare an earnings release. The three primary points of the NIRI guidelines are:

- Include both a complete income statement and a complete balance sheet.
- Put GAAP earnings up front and before pro forma results.
- Include key information in the earnings announcement.

A complete explanation of these guidelines can be found on NIRI's website (www.niri.org).

Timing the release: To give investors the opportunity to absorb and evaluate the information, earnings releases are generally scheduled outside the trading hours of the major stock exchanges, that is, not between 9:30 A.M. and 4:00 P.M. Eastern Standard Time. There are two schools of thought about how best to achieve that objective: (1) before the market opens or (2) after it closes.

- *Before the market opens:* The more traditional approach, a pre-market announcement has the benefit of coming at the beginning of the day for financial reporters. With a full day, reporters can gather opinion from financial experts and assess how the marketplace is reacting to the news. However, during busy periods, early releases can lead to a logjam at the services which distribute press releases, and delay the company's news. This can be important when positive earnings need to be reported.

- *After the market closes:* Releasing earnings after the markets close limits the amount of time that financial media have before the deadline to file stories for the next day's paper. That in turn limits their ability to get third-party comment on the results. The real market reaction to the news won't be known until the end of the following day. Nevertheless, some companies, particularly ones in the high-tech arena or with West Coast headquarters, view an after-the-close timing as more equitable for investors concentrated on the West Coast—for whom a pre-market release would come at around 5:00 A.M. in their time zone.

Providing further elaboration on the results: Conference calls and webcasts typically follow earnings releases, either later in that day or the following day. These channels ensure equitable access for all investors to management's insights, and the SEC has even spoken of conference calls as part of a "best practices" approach to announcing earnings. Investor response to both the facts discussed during a call and the way management handles its presentation and discussion of the numbers and the business can have a quick and profound impact on stock price. Managements consequently devote a great deal of time and attention to preparing for these events.

In the past, many IR executives and their bosses would try to prevent reporters from joining analysts' meetings or conference calls. But in the post–Reg FD environment, reporters are now embraced as an instrument of disclosure when they listen in to the call.

The whole process of releasing earnings has become more transparent in this Reg FD–inspired environment. On a practical level, scheduling earnings conference calls and giving investors adequate advanced notice of them has led companies to issue advisories a week or so in advance. These advisories make it much easier for financial reporters to track developments and schedule their reporting.

The media can provide even more avenues to broad dissemination of a company's insights and guidance. Some CEOs routinely take advantage of interview opportunities on CNBC, Bloomberg, CNN, *Nightly Business Report*, FOX, or other outlets.

3. Reporting material developments

In line with the strictures of Reg FD, companies have an obligation to report publicly when a significant business development occurs that causes what is known as a "material" impact on operations, or when a review of past accounts shows an error or omission that will lead to an adjustment of the books. The underlying question is in determining whether something is or isn't "material."

Defining "material":   One rule of thumb that is often cited is the "5% rule"—which suggests that if a development will impact earnings by 5 percent plus or minus, then it is "material." In addition, the SEC has a list of formal requirements for "material" events that automatically trigger a need for disclosure:

- Change in control of the company
- Acquisition or disposition of a significant amount of assets
- Filing for bankruptcy or receivership
- Change in the company's certifying accountant
- Resignation of a company director
- Change in the company's fiscal year

But other developments can also be considered "material" if they significantly change the company's reported financial position. The SEC's website (www.sec.gov) discusses at length the process of determining "materiality." Cautioning against relying too heavily on numerical "rules of thumb," the SEC staff offers this suggestion for guidance: "A matter is 'material' if there is a substantial likelihood that a reasonable person would consider it important." Company legal counsel will ultimately make the final determination of whether an event is material.

"Pre-announcing":   Mindful of the Reg FD obligations to broadly disclose "material" changes, companies have increasingly chosen to err on the side of caution. Coupled with the heightened trend of the markets to punish the price of stocks that surprise investors with poor performance, companies have dramatically increased their use of public "profit warnings" in advance of their quarterly earnings release. This practice is called "pre-announcing," and occurs when a company concludes that its earnings will not meet the "consensus estimate." These types of announcements reflect the evolutionary change that is taking place in the reporting of material financial developments.

4. Announcing executive changes

When announcing any executive appointment, from CEO on down to sales manager, your executive-change press release should:

- Convey how this person's new position fits with the underlying business strategy.
- Show how this appointment either contributes to programs that are working well, or sets the stage for change where it's needed.

What to include:

- The individual's new position/title
- Where the person comes from—either prior post within the organization, or previous employer
- Who this person is replacing and where the replaced person is going and why (which can be a short sentence)
- Why the replaced person left (something you may wish to fudge with a platitude like "left to pursue other interests")
- Quotes from appropriate levels (typically the appointee's new boss mentions one or two significant details of the individual's background or past work, and states why this should mean the person will be good for the company in this new capacity)
- The ages of the executives (some publications simply will not print news of executive changes without that detail, just as some obituary pages won't run a death listing without reporting the cause of death)

Where to place: Be realistic about the placement possibilities for any specific appointment.

- Trade publications, city and regional business magazines, and local dailies typically have their own columns dedicated to executive changes and will cover a broad spectrum of appointments from CEO on down.
- National business publications and news networks consider change in the C-suite (your top management—CEO, CFO, etc.) and boards of major companies to be newsworthy.
- But for companies below the *Fortune* 1000, or for titles below the level of senior vice president, national coverage is certainly not guaranteed.
- You can enhance your chance of successful placement by making sure your announcement is sent both to the reporter who regularly covers your company and to the attention of the specific column that tracks executive changes.

II. TRANSFORMATIONAL EVENTS

"Transformational events" are those that go beyond the routine kinds of communications and disclosures covered in the first part of this chapter. They involve significant change that may affect the fundamental course of a company's existence. The impact on stock price can be expected to be dramatic and quick. These events include (1) mergers and acquisitions, (2) restructurings, and (3) corporate malfeasance. By definition, these are "material" events, but their impact can be orders of magnitude greater than that of garden-variety material items. They usually affect a wide range of the company's constituencies, and automatically appeal to the media's interest.

Keep in mind three key points when communicating about transformational events:

- *Handle with care.* Because this is material news, all strictures about Reg FD and selective disclosure must apply to its release. Given the likely moves in the stock, your planning, implementation, and conduct will probably come under great scrutiny if any suspicion of insider trading arises. Communication professionals have faced criminal charges for violating disclosure requirements.

- *Be sensitive to the information needs of all your audiences.* Your shareholders will be covered if you follow Reg FD, but what about your key customers and suppliers? And don't forget about employees. If they learn from the morning newspaper or local radio that their company has been sold, your employees will feel slighted. It may take a Herculean effort, but timing employee meetings or internal announcements, via email or voicemail, to coincide with the news release can address this issue.

- *Look to the future.* Whatever the news—merger or bankruptcy—it is important to convey your vision of the future at the point of the announcement. What are the positives? What will be the practical changes?

1. Announcing mergers and acquisitions

The most common form of corporate transformation is when one company buys another or is itself bought. Such acquisitions usually mean that one company and its management team and corporate culture will ultimately dominate the new organization. But for a variety of reasons, largely involving internal or community perceptions, these combinations are often talked about as "mergers," a term that suggests a less aggressive combination of mutual strengths.

Elements of a merger announcement: Merger announcements should include the following items:

- Names of the parties involved
- Price paid or other financial arrangements
- How the transaction will be funded—whether cash, stock, a combination of both
- Benefits of the combination for varied parties: shareholders, employees, consumers, customers, and communities
- Management for the new entity
- Impact on earnings—timeframe for the deal to be accretive
- Regulatory concerns, and how they will be addressed
- Background on the deal principals
- Identities of key advisors
- Timetable for completing the deal

Tactical concerns for merger announcements: Given the range of interested parties, communicating details of mergers presents special challenges.

- *The benefits balance:* The most difficult part of organizing a merger announcement is likely to be striking a balance within the "benefits" section, where the vision of the future is laid out. For shareholders to realize their maximum benefit, the company may need to focus on "operating synergies" of the deal that will only be achieved through layoffs within duplicated areas of the business. The shareholder benefit will come at the expense of some employees.
- *News embargoes:* Taking advantage of the Reg FD media carve-out, one tactic that can be used to get prominent attention for messages about a merger is to negotiate "exclusives" or "embargoes." The goal is to secure a positive story in a prominent daily on the morning that

you otherwise announce your deal. Because this story would run before the markets open, your strategic messages appear separate from any discussion of how investor response impacted your share price.

To get the exclusive, you offer special access—perhaps to the CEOs on both sides of a deal—to key journalists in return for guarantees that might include working only off the interviews, not pursuing other sources, and withholding the story from publication until a set time. Journalists for their part are willing to engineer such quid-pro-quos. Access to information is their goal, and being offered the day's "hot story" makes them look good with their editors.

But there can be significant negatives to this approach. Journalists who are not offered the same deal will feel undercut, which could inspire them to hunt for negative opinions about your news. Hometown media can be particularly upset by national exclusives. Employees who see the news "in the paper" before hearing from their own company may conclude that management is more interested in communicating with investors than with workers.

2. Announcing restructurings

While mergers by their nature are generally perceived as positive news, that's not the case for a company announcing a Chapter 11 filing or other form of reorganization or restructuring. Restructuring involves retrenchment and usually provokes uncertainty about the future. These events are often accompanied by a hint of failure or at least missed objectives. Such events raise questions of confidence in management.

Companies facing these situations have to allay a wide range of fears and communicate what certainties there are. They must explain to employees why they should stick with the organization. Creditors, customers, and suppliers must be persuaded that—whatever the short-term impact—this is a positive for them over the long haul. Shareholders, who generally see some of the value of their investment disappear (although stocks of most distressed companies have already plummeted well before this stage), might be offered some solace.

Typically, such messages should include these kinds of statements:

- Despite the retrenchment, the core of the company remains in business.
- Payroll will be met (for some defined period of time).
- Management is taking every step possible to preserve the largest number of jobs for as long as possible.
- Customer needs will be served.

3. Disclosing malfeasance

Stuff happens. Businesses can be the victims of rogue employees who embezzle funds, who overstate their personal performance (and thus the company's results), or who simply have been incompetent in the performance of their duties. When malfeasance occurs at the highest levels of the company, it can literally tear the organization apart and turn the corporate culture on its head.

How you respond once you learn about it will influence how the media and other audiences will respond.

Some of the key elements of disclosing malfeasance are:

- Demonstrate that management responded quickly to the situation.
- Show how appropriate responsibility has been taken to fix the situation.
- Confirm that the company is informing or working with authorities as appropriate.
- Detail how the company is investigating the specifics of the incident.
- Demonstrate how management is moving to protect the interests of employees shareholders, customers, and community.
- Clarify what procedures will be implemented to prevent recurrence.
- Indicate how the responsible parties have been dealt with or disciplined.

Companies can expect to confront some level of malfeasance over the course of time. Controlling it and limiting news exposure is critical. When problems of malfeasance call into question an organization's integrity and threaten its existence, the situation can evolve into a crisis. The next chapter examines corporate crises and discusses a range of strategies for dealing with them.

Chapter Summary: FINANCIAL MEDIA COMMUNICATIONS		
Type of event	**Subject of communication**	**Comments**
Routine	Earnings	• Generally issued two to three weeks after the close of the quarter. • Usually followed by conference calls and webcasts.
	"Material" developments	• Issued when significant impact occurs on operations or financial conditions. • Often used in advance of weak earnings announcement to forewarn investors.
	Executive changes	• Should convey link to underlying business strategy. • Will be met with higher interest if senior executives are involved.
Transformational	Merger and acquisition	• Needs to balance benefits involving a range of affected parties. • Should show strategic fit.
	Restructuring	• Should mitigate uncertainty among affected parties. • Must communicate long-term benefits.
	Malfeasance	• Should demonstrate that appropriate measures have been undertaken to resolve the current situation and prevent recurrence. • Should be portrayed as atypical.

CHAPTER V OUTLINE

I. Understanding the media in crises
1. Analyze crises
2. Understand the media's motivations

II. Choosing a response strategy
1. Free to attack
2. Forced to defend
3. Forced to avoid
4. Free to ignore
5. Problem solving: the overlooked strategy

III. Developing tactics for handling the media
1. Avoid committing fundamental errors
2. Consider timing issues
3. Choose your communication channel

CHAPTER V

Batten Down the Hatches: Handling the Media in a Crisis

Crises are characterized by fast-moving developments and an element of danger—to physical well-being or reputation. What creates "crisis" conditions is the immediate or potential loss of control over the situation and its outcome. Faced with a crisis, you may be overwhelmed with cascading and often contradictory tasks and responsibilities. It's difficult to act strategically when minute-by-minute demands require a host of immediate decisions. The media's presence adds yet another degree of complexity to such situations.

This chapter examines ways to interact with media in the development and coverage of a corporate crisis. It will assess reasons why the media cover crises, offer a range of strategies for crisis coverage, and provide a set of tactical responses that can be used to handle the media during a crisis.

I. UNDERSTANDING THE MEDIA IN CRISES

The media can act as a conduit to important audiences during a crisis. On the other hand, if their interests and needs are not taken into account as a crisis unfolds, the media can become an obstacle to the delivery of messages you need conveyed. With the advent of nonstop electronic news coverage, the forces driving media coverage have intensified. This reality means that dealing with the press demands an octopus-like outreach: staying in touch with news sources, keeping tabs on coverage, using the Internet, and answering a multitude of requests for information. This section covers how to analyze a crisis and understand the media's motivations during a crisis.

1. Analyze crises.

This section categorizes and highlights examples of well-known crises. Undoubtedly, each crisis will be comprised of its own peculiarities and dynamics; however, knowing the commonalities among them will be useful when you examine how to deal with the media during a specific crisis.

Distinguish between problems and crises.   Organizations always face challenges to their operations and financial health. Managers get paid to anticipate and mitigate such developments. Although these situations may create serious repercussions for an organization, the problems that turn into true crises need to be separated from problems more commonly encountered by managers.

- *Problems:* Every business function encounters serious problems over the course of time. For example, Marketing faces a bump in the road when a new-product roll-out gets caught in an unexpected patent infringement suit; the R&D department discovers that critical test results have been fudged by a technician hoping to look good in a supervisor's eyes; Treasury is hit with a rogue employee who's been embezzling for years. Clearly, these are problems, but are they crises?

- *Crises:* When faced with a business problem, ask yourself the following set of questions. Does the business problem threaten to severely affect the organization's (1) normal workflow and distract senior management? (2) financial well-being? (3) image and reputation in the eyes of critical constituencies?

If you answer "yes" to all of them, your problem is likely a crisis in the making and a crisis usually requires such a trifecta of complications.

- *Severity:* But how serious is the potential crisis? Consider how the U.S. National Weather Service assigns severity to hurricanes: depending upon the storm's wind speed and the probability of property damage and flooding, it assigns a numerical ranking ranging from 1 to 5 (most devastating). Organizational crises can be assessed in a similar way. And like a Category 1 or 2 hurricane that can suddenly become a far more dangerous threat and evolve into a Category 4 or 5 monster, so organizational crises can grow and spiral into unexpected proportions. You need to be prepared to react appropriately along that curve. Like an increase in a hurricane's wind speed, the media's presence during a crisis raises the potential for greater organizational harm.

Consider the causes of crises. Crises tend to fall into four categories of causation: financial, litigation, public opinion, or event. Understanding which category of crisis you face can help you determine whom you need to contact, the kind of media source best suited to delivering your message, and the other key constituents you want to reach immediately. Because crises by definition involve volatility, the nature of a crisis may shift from one category to another. These shifts occur when a new set of stakeholders become affected or concerned and when the media tracks this newfound interest.

- *Financial crises:* If a company is facing bankruptcy, hostile takeover, a strike, or massive employee layoffs, the crisis originates in the financial arena. Financial media and business reporters will naturally have the most initial interest in these kinds of circumstances. However, when jobs, taxes, or real estate are at stake, media interest quickly spreads to local radio, TV, and newspapers. Examples of notable financial crises include: The Salomon Brothers Treasury Bill crisis, 1991–1992; Drexel-Burnham insider trading crisis, 1986–1990; and Enron, 2001–2002. Each of these crises shifted into litigation and the forum of public opinion.

- *Litigation crises:* Given the enormous number of legal suits in the United States, most such cases remain out of the media's eye. Nevertheless, when the courts form the battleground, the adversarial nature of the legal system lends itself to vocal, antagonistic claims from plaintive parties. If the lawsuit captures the media's interest, or if either side's intransigence attracts attention, then the crisis may be on its way to the front page. Examples of such crises include: the Dow-Corning breast implant crisis, 1989–2001; the Microsoft–U.S. Government lawsuit; and the Ford–Firestone SUV rollover crisis, 2000–2002. Each of these crises shifted to the financial category and the forum of public opinion.

- *Forum of public opinion crises:* Some business issues become popular causes. These causes gain strength over time, become widely reported, force sides to be formed, and foment the need for legislative action. Frequently, these causes arise when an interested party, or constituency, perceives an issue in either of two ways: (1) *Conception of risk:* When the issue's advocacy group feels threatened, it may enlist the media to publicize its sense of fear. Genetically modified food, nuclear power, smoking, and "second hand" smoke are examples of risk-based issues. (2) *Conception of rights:* When an issue speaks to a constituency's sense of moral or legal rights, it may find a ready ear in sympathetic media outlets. The animal rights movement, multinational use of Third-World labor, and the patients' rights movement exemplify this kind of issue. Examples of issue-driven crises that originated in the forum of public opinion include Nike's use of Third-World factory production, 1990–2001; Monsanto and the production of genetically modified grain, 1985–2002; and Nestlé's marketing of infant formula in Third-World countries, 1977–1990. Each of these crises shifted to the litigation zone.

- *Event-based crises:* Crises can be caused by physical events. Fires, earthquakes, hurricanes, accidents, contamination, or criminal actions may precipitate crises. Examples of such crises include Three Mile Island, 1979; *Exxon-Valdez* oil spill 1990; and Coke contamination in Europe, 1999. These crises shifted to the financial sector, the litigation sector, and the forum of public opinion.

Control damage.   Crises frequently spin out of control. As indicated above, some crises will shift from one category to another. What may have begun as a financial crisis can lurch into litigation as the company suddenly faces a flurry of lawsuits; the interest of the public may be aroused and then the crisis shifts to the forum of public opinion. As a result, a different set of media outlets will take notice and shine their lights on the company.

In most crises, a primary objective is to keep the situation anchored in one of the categories and reduce the likelihood that it will shift to another. Crisis response will still be a difficult task, but managing that response can be a more feasible process.

2. Understand the media's motivations.

To effectively handle the media in a crisis, you must analyze how the media views its role in such situations. With that understanding comes the recognition that if you are handling a crisis properly, the media may be one of your most important allies, and not something to avoid at all costs. In other words, you want the media to be your mouthpiece instead of the monkey on your back.

The media are not a single monolith: even in the worst crises involving life-threatening dangers, some will behave responsibly, some irresponsibly. The good news is that the public has as little stomach for irresponsible media as it does for CEOs who cook their companies' books. Your circumstances may require you to focus your attention on the responsible media who, if you deal with them fairly, can provide an important avenue for conveying your story.

Five key drivers spur the media's coverage in a crisis. Understanding these drivers—and tailoring your crisis response to accommodate them—will help you deal with the media and speed crisis resolution.

Informing: Fundamentally, informing is the media's business—telling the old "Five Ws": Who, What, When, Where, and Why. Failing to respond to questions concerning these basic tenets of information is a prescription for confrontation with reporters who aren't being given enough data to do their jobs. Therefore, be wary of responding with variations of "I don't know who did it, but it wasn't us," or "we can't be sure what went wrong, what time it happened, or where it really started." Such sidestepping leads reporters to look more deeply into the situation. And you can expect that they will go looking for information from other sources.

Conveying information and aid: In physical crises—such as natural disasters, major explosions, and chemical spills that threaten communities—the public and the government rely on the media, especially electronic media, to convey vital life-saving information to the public. If an explosion occurs at your facility, the media can help you explain that the effects are confined to the plant grounds, and there is no need for area residents to flee. Or if the opposite is true, the media can help you clear the surrounding area and limit public exposure, and perhaps your organization's liability.

Titillating: The downside of media coverage is the press' tendency to play to the worst of tabloid journalism's excesses. This driver occurs when the "media pack" becomes the equivalent of the mob shouting for the ledge-sitter to "Jump!" The motivation is to create a visceral thrill from the misfortune of others. This form of journalism has plenty of critics. But keep in mind that censure by editorialists doesn't seem to diminish ratings for sensational coverage. News directors at competing stations will still risk the wrath of police chiefs by flying so many news choppers above a "breaking story" that they impede the police. The voyeurs are out there, and you need to be prepared to deal with them.

Assigning blame: At the end of the day, or the news cycle, one question the media want answered is, "Who's to blame?" Exposing "liars" or fingering the "villains" is the Holy Grail of journalism. Blame is one thing that the press wants to find and companies want to avoid. Later in this chapter, we examine alternative approaches to take when confronted with the blame-seeking press.

"Earning their Pulitzer":   Sometimes those handling crises have to deal with a fifth driver of media action: "Earning their Pulitzer." The national exposure that can accompany an individual journalist's coverage of a crisis can be a springboard for job offers and career advancement. The onslaught of front-page articles creates another kind of media frenzy, and the story will often migrate rapidly from print to broadcast form.

II. CHOOSING A RESPONSE STRATEGY

An organization under intense media scrutiny can respond with a variety of overall strategies, as illustrated in the model on the next page. Use this model to choose a strategy based on two decisions. First, decide how aggressive you choose to be: the aggressive response is shown on the top and the passive reaction is shown at the bottom. Second, decide how free you feel about your options: "free to choose" what to do is shown on the left and "forced to react" is shown on the right.

Determining which course of action to undertake will require an examination of many factors: the organization's strengths and vulnerabilities, the nature of the crisis, the validity of the organization's position, the timeframe involved, and the potential for governmental or judicial response. Senior management will often assemble a crisis task force—whose members should include communications and legal executives—to assess the organization's options. (The bibliography on pages 118–119 lists several books concerned with crisis management in general, and they can provide further detail on the decision-making process.)

Based on those decisions, four initial strategies emerge: "free to attack," "forced to defend," "forced to avoid," and "free to ignore." Let's consider each of those strategies in turn; at the end of the chapter, we'll look at a more creative fifth option as well.

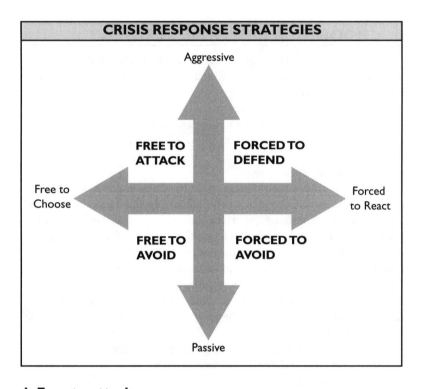

1. Free to attack

FREE TO ATTACK	
Why:	Unfair blame needs to be rebutted
How:	Attack accusers; attack the media for inaccuracy; use sympathetic media outlets to force other groups to defend themselves
Advantages:	Shifts responsibility; redirects stakeholder attention
Disadvantages:	Creates more attention among media or investigators; heightens public interest; sets up potential for later exposure of wrongdoing

"Free to attack" is the strategy to use if you have a strong case to make. You may feel outraged by media coverage or you may think you have a story to tell that can redirect the brunt of the media coverage. The company takes an offensive strategy, with a corresponding impression of verve and confidence. An attack strategy can work— but the company must have a highly credible story to tell. The underlying facts must support the message and tactics employed must take into account the culpability lurking beneath the accusations.

In the 1990s, this strategy was adopted with varying degrees of success. The usual tactical weapon involves threat of lawsuit. Here are some notable examples of companies engaging in this strategy:

***General Motors vs. NBC* (1993):** NBC's *Dateline*, a television magazine program, broadcast footage ostensibly showing a Chevrolet pickup explode as a result of gas tanks positioned beneath the driving cab. GM learned that the sequence had been staged, using incendiary devices to set off the explosions. GM obtained outtakes, called a news conference, and exposed the deception. NBC apologized publicly and fired those responsible.

***Chiquita vs. Cincinnati Inquirer* (1997–99):** When an investigative reporter obtained information about Chiquita's business practices by gaining unauthorized access to computer files and voicemail, the company sued the newspaper for theft, won its case, and received a front-page apology from the publisher.

***Food Lion vs. ABC* (1992–97):** Using hidden cameras and an "undercover" employee, ABC's news magazine *Nightline* showed how the supermarket chain was cutting corners on food safety to ensure higher profit margins. The company counterattacked and sued the network, claiming the network producer obtained employment under false premises and illegally shot footage on private property. The case dragged on for years; the supermarket chain lost money, its stock dropped, and it finally lost its case. It took years to regain market share.

***Mitsubishi Motors vs. EEOC* (1996):** Female assembly line workers charged the company with sexual discrimination and the federal government's Equal Employment Opportunity Commission brought a class action suit on the workers' behalf. The company counterattacked by bussing hundreds of plant workers to the EEOC's Chicago office to protest the suit. Press coverage intensified, a U.S. boycott was announced, anti-company protestors made national news in Japan. The company finally settled the lawsuit nearly a year later, but sales in the United States suffered from the negative publicity.

2. Forced to defend

FORCED TO DEFEND	
Why:	Actions in question are justified; no choice but to defend the com pany's position against critics
How:	Make spokespeople available; provide background information; educate reporters about the situation; reach out to potential allies through media reportage
Advantages:	Allows the company to justify its decisions in a public manner; may improve employee morale
Disadvantages:	May cause some to view company as defensive

Another strategy comes about when you decide your choices are limited and you must react. In such instances, you will be "forced to defend" your actions. For such approaches to be successful, the company needs to obtain a receptive hearing from the media or, at least, get its version of events delivered in a credible context. Companies with poor media relations, or those that rarely work with reporters or avoid interaction on a regular basis, will find this a difficult objective to achieve, because this strategy is ultimately a reactive one. "We were justified" responds to accusations of the opposite. After all, the company's message will be pitted against a chorus of critics, who frequently will receive equal billing in the press.

Examples of the "forced to defend" strategy abound, and here are some well-known campaigns:

***Disney Company vs. Land Preservationists* (1993–94):**   When the Disney Company announced plans for an American history theme park near the Civil War battle site of Manassas, a coalition of opposing groups organized against it. Disney executives were forced to defend the project, asserting financial benefits for the region and promising fidelity to the historical record. Faced with vocal and influential opposition, the company backed down and withdrew its plans.

*Nike vs. **Human Rights Activists** (**1990–98**):* Accused of under-paying and exploiting labor in the Third World, the company defended its business strategy by claiming financial benefits for the shoe workers. Later, it defended its actions by claiming it did not directly run the sneaker factories. Eventually, the company adopted a problem-solving strategy (to be discussed later in this section) instituting a series of remedies, including overseers and improved accountability.

*Microsoft vs. U.S. (**1998–2002**):* Microsoft used this strategy in its battle with the federal government over charges of monopolistic business practices. The company felt it had to defend its business model and practices to maintain market position.

3. Forced to avoid

FORCED TO AVOID	
Why:	External factors prevent the company from communicating actively
How:	Spokesperson avoids commenting to the press but may express regret; company asks for patience through media interviews
Advantages:	Strategy reduces potential for misunderstood statements; may reduce later legal liability
Disadvantages:	Company likely perceived to be holding out information; media may assign guilt; may provoke more scrutiny as the curiosity factor heightens

This approach positions the company in passive mode, where circumstances force a kind of silence. Because of extenuating circumstances or lack of information, this strategy is most frequently framed by the message "We are unable to comment at this time." Legal departments will often counsel a company to use this approach since it offers apparent protection from miscues, misquotes, and the like, which might subsequently be used against the firm.

However, even when justified legally, this strategy puts the company in a vulnerable position. In the court of public opinion, silence or the refusal to defend oneself is equated with guilt. Meanwhile, any number of other interested parties will be sure to voice their reactions and the media will have little compunction about offering them their chance to do so. This barrage of commentary becomes particularly galling for companies when unattributed "sources" are used, often lawyers who are involved on the opposing side of the litigation.

Bank of New York (1999):   When the Bank of New York was charged with money laundering for organized crime, the firm adopted this strategy. However, information was leaked to the press, apparently from those close to the investigation. The case grew more complex and coverage increased as reporters searched for the names of responsible parties. The Bank of New York, with its patrician reputation in the crucible, suffered from media overexposure and tabloid-like investigation.

TWA (1996):   In 1996, TWA management found itself in an excruciating position in the aftermath of the crash of Flight 800 over Long Island Sound. With its CEO in Europe and unavailable for immediate comment, local management were unable to respond to media (and family) inquiries concerning the flight manifest and other crucial details. Mayor Rudolph Guiliani publicly castigated the company for its inability (or unwillingness) to immediately communicate in the hours following the disaster. The company suffered grievous reputational and financial loss from this incident: investor confidence never recovered, nor did the company's stock price, even after a succession of new CEOs were put in place. It could be argued that TWA's eventual demise can be traced to its actions and lack of communication in July 1996.

4. Free to ignore

FREE TO IGNORE	
Why:	The company feels impervious to media-generated harm.
How:	Avoid media access entirely
Advantages:	Eliminates distractions and complications of media interaction
Disadvantages:	Company perceived to be arrogant; media may assign guilt; may provoke more scrutiny as the curiosity factor heightens.

If a company believes it cannot be harmed by media coverage, then it may opt for staying entirely out of view and not making spokespersons available. This strategy has often been adopted by industrial suppliers or non-consumer-based companies. Privately held companies also often believe that this response to media inquiry is the best: the absence of shareholders eliminates an important constituency that often demands information or can be influenced by media coverage. Companies with virtual monopolies over certain services or products also may feel insulated from any effects. As a final example, international companies with U.S.-based subsidiaries sometimes adopt this approach: their cultural misreading of the media's role in the U.S. business scene leads them to believe that what works in the home country—silence—will work well here.

The danger behind this strategy lies in its assumptions of insularity and strength. Most companies in fact do need to consider the secondary effects that result from the media's coverage of its actions. Privately held companies, for example, do not exist under veiled cover. They ultimately have customers who are susceptible to media influence.

For years, "no comment" was the norm. During the 1980s, companies felt particularly free to ignore media inquiry. Hooker Chemical and its no-comment policy in the wake of the Love Canal environmental crisis is a prime example. By the time the company could respond to allegations and lawsuits, its credibility was profoundly undermined.

As the intensity of the subject under investigation heightens, "no comment" becomes equated in the media's vocabulary with admitted guilt. The refusal to comment also brings out the journalist's urge to dig deeper. You won't comment? Well, no doubt your competitor will; perhaps a public official or an analyst, eager to make an impression with their constituencies, will be happy to comment. Unanswered, these third-party comments will accumulate, potentially affecting image and reputation.

5. Problem solving: the overlooked strategy

PROBLEM SOLVING	
Why:	By the company's communicating willingness to engage in a solution, the media will likely move on to other stories, reducing pressure and distraction on the company.
How:	Engage key media sources to explain decision; use Internet to reach stakeholders; consider holding a press conference.
Advantages:	Impression of commitment may preserve reputation; risk of ongoing media inquiry lessened; employee morale may be improved
Disadvantages:	Risk of follow-up in the event expectations are not satisfied; threat to reputation if company seen as saying one thing and doing another.

The most overlooked strategy? The problem-solving approach. Whenever a company can position its response as a meaningful effort to acknowledge and correct some phenomenon that has led to the crisis, media coverage will become more favorable and stakeholder impressions will, in the long run, not impugn the company's reputation.

The figure on the facing page illustrates how this approach can be placed on the original model's horizontal axis spanning "free to respond" to "forced to respond." Thus, a company can be proactive—"free to solve" (for example, a company appointing an outsider to oversee new personnel policies in the face of federal discrimination suits), or apologetic in scope—"forced to solve" (a company acknowledging system or worker error as the cause of an accident).

A problem-solving strategy, however, rarely comes to mind for most managers. Reasons range from concerns about admitting to legal liability to the cultural reluctance of competitive, success-oriented business executives to admit error. Yet in the aftermath of a crisis, the least difficult job a company may have is to show how it will make amends, take steps to ameliorate stakeholder concerns, or simply apologize. How real is this specter of subsequent legal proceedings that paralyzes many a senior manager? As one crisis counselor comments, "Where have damages ever been higher as a result of a company's contrition? I have never seen it." In many instances, companies would be better served to portray themselves as constructive parties to a potential solution than self-righteous warriors fighting off media attacks.

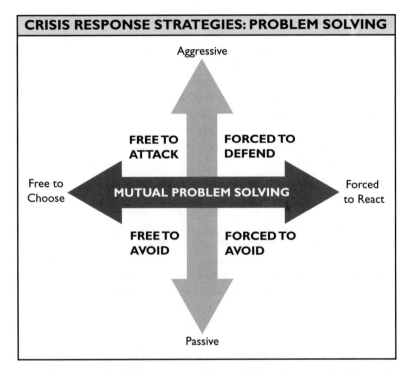

CRISIS RESPONSE STRATEGIES: PROBLEM SOLVING

Aggressive

FREE TO ATTACK   FORCED TO DEFEND

Free to Choose   MUTUAL PROBLEM SOLVING   Forced to React

FREE TO AVOID   FORCED TO AVOID

Passive

Problem-Solving responses can be proactive or apologetic. Here are some notable examples of this approach:

***Texaco vs. EEOC* (1996):**   After allegations of racial discrimination were published nationally, CEO Peter Budjar pledged an impartial investigation, brought in a respected outside jurist to conduct it, and publicly acknowledged the need for improvement in hiring and promotion procedures. Media coverage, which was intense, waned.

***Salomon Brothers vs. U.S. Dept. of Justice* (1992):**   In the wake of the Treasury Bill scandal that forced the firm's leading executives to resign, acting CEO Warren Buffet acknowledged problems, revamped management, and communicated commitment to change. Within a short period of time, press coverage shifted to the more positive story of the firm's revitalization.

***Heinz vs. Earth Island* (1990):**   Faced with a nationwide boycott of its canned fish products, the company pledged it would purchase only tuna that did not imperil dolphins and promised to lead a world-wide effort to reduce dolphin deaths as a result of commercial fishing. Increased sales reversed its precipitous decline.

Although each of these five strategies may represent an appropriate response to a crisis, it's also important to realize that shifts in strategy may occur—or become necessary. Most commonly, strategic shifts will move toward "mutual problem solving." For example, in 1996, the EEOC sued Mitsubishi over sexual discrimination in the workplace. As mentioned, the company first responded in a "free to attack" mode. After several months, however, the results were an increase in negative media coverage, a U.S. boycott, and protests at Tokyo corporate headquarters. The company changed course, brought in new management to the U.S. subsidiary, and moved into the "mutual problem solving" mode. It appointed an outside overseer to examine and change employment policies.

Shifts can also occur in other sectors. A. H. Robins, makers of the controversial Dalkon Shield employed a "free to ignore" strategy when confronted with scores of reports that the birth control device was malfunctioning and causing harm. When media attention heightened and lawsuits were about to be filed, it shifted to "free to attack" and attempted to vilify the women who brought suit, alleging an assortment of unsavory personal behaviors as the cause of the malfunctions. This damaged Robins' credibility and reputation immensely. The company went into bankruptcy, later to be acquired by a competitor.

Advantages and Disadvantages: CRISIS RESPONSE STRATEGIES		
Strategy	**Advantages**	**Disadvantages**
Free to Attack	• Puts opponents and media on defensive.	• Media may search for wrongdoing and expose it to public.
Free to Avoid	• Eliminates media as a distraction.	• Media may dig deeper and force new revelations.
Forced to Defend	• Justifies course of action to key stakeholders.	• Company can be seen as defensive and inflexible.
Forced to Avoid	• May reduce legal liability.	• Media may assign guilt.
Mutual Problem Solving	• Creates impression of commitment and care.	• Heightened expectations may result in criticism if follow-through is insufficient.

III. DEVELOPING TACTICS FOR HANDLING THE MEDIA

Once you have chosen your strategy, you will need to assess which tactics will best help you reach your objectives. Choosing the right channel to convey messages is essential and determining appropriate timing becomes vital. From an understanding of the media's motivations and incentives, you will be better equipped to meet the media's demand for information during a crisis. Chapter I provided an overview of the channels available to communicate with the media, and Chapter II offered insights into applying those channels effectively. You may need to use many—if not all—of those channels in a crisis. But before choosing the appropriate channel, it's important to review what you should not do—and why.

1. Avoid committing fundamental errors.

Regardless of your strategy, keep in mind the following provisos.

Do not lie to the press.   Lying to the press is like throwing blood into the shark tank. Although there are many good reasons that organizations shouldn't lie in their communications, perhaps the most crass is that with the media, your lie is most likely going to be found out—and you will pay dearly for it later. Beechnut found out the hard way when its "100%" apple juice was found to actually contain a cocktail of sugar and water and very little real fruit juice. The company was fined $2 million and its president pleaded guilty to felony charges, getting docked an extra $100,000 for good measure. More recently, cover-ups and distortions emanating from companies such as Enron and Worldcom were revealed in the press and took their toll on the viability of these corporations.

Assess the reporter's motivation.   For example, beware of a reporter who phones to say, "Your company is doing such a good job (for consumers/handling this situation/etc.) that we want to come over and interview you at your plant." Shocking as it may be, reporters have been known to lie to get a story or access to one. Do your due diligence: know who you're dealing with and how they've treated others in the past; try to assess their real motivation.

Use the right spokesperson.   Never commit to putting others from your organization on the phone or on camera before you know if they are trained and capable. The most well-intentioned and responsible executives may develop stage fright on camera—and their nervous appearance could give a false impression that they have something to hide.

Once your news is out, you may want to bring in your heavy hitters, or maybe the relief pitchers, to help provide context that shapes the story. For example, to ensure the best possible stories in one or two key business and trade media, you may want to provide a more personal touch from the top; your CEO's personal stamp may be needed. In another instance, perhaps the bulk of press callers could be referred to the CEO's quote that you've included in the press release. Or it may help advance your strategy to grant access to a mid-level insider who is knowledgeable about a particular process or activity, such as your senior environmental or safety officer.

Do not say "no comment."   This phrase has come to be associated with admission of guilt. There are more elegant, and less negative, ways to say that you're not able to respond to specific questions at this time. It's far better to provide a sense of the process involved. For example, "The company is investigating as we speak, and our senior staff is hard at work trying to get to the bottom of the immediate problem," or "We're committed to making information known when we in fact receive it. We're in the process of finding out exactly what happened."

Avoid the blame trap.   Blame is one thing that the press wants to find and companies want to avoid. For many organizations, the instinctive response to accusations of blame is first to deny and then later find a scapegoat. Yet nothing sets off a "feeding frenzy" among the press more quickly than an attempt to shift blame that doesn't stand up to scrutiny. The media are trained to smell a phony story or a weak excuse.

Your response has to balance responsible behavior with protecting corporate reputation. Those are not mutually exclusive concepts. While it seems counterintuitive to some people, accepting "responsibility" can be different from "taking the blame." It can also be the best way to move forward to address the real crisis, and at the same time develop support from the general public, the media, and other key audiences. But even within organizations, participants on the inside can begin to waste valuable time because they're scrambling to place or avoid blame instead of first resolving and stabilizing the crisis.

Classic examples of that principle at work is the contrast between the handling of two similar crises by two oil companies.

- *Exxon Valdez disaster:* More than a decade after the oil spill in Prince William Sound in Alaska, Exxon still is vilified by many for its mishandling of that crisis. Seemingly at every turn, Exxon's response was hostile and combative. First, the company tried to assign blame to the single individual of the "drunken" boat captain, ignoring the question of whether that meant Exxon had put too much responsibility in one set of shaky hands, and without adequate backup systems. This "Exxon as victim" positioning backfired. Then, the company appeared to fight cleanup efforts and vilify anyone with concerns about the pollution of the sound, creating fresh enemies at every turn. Each of those strategies ensured that Exxon's name would forever be associated with a well-covered disaster.

- *Ashland Oil spill:* In contrast, few today remember that Ashland Oil experienced its own spill crisis, when 700,000 gallons of diesel fuel poured from a ruptured Ashland tank and was carried by the Monongahela River into the Ohio River, threatening the drinking water of Pittsburgh and an estimated one million people in Pennsylvania, West Virginia, and Ohio. Because Ashland's CEO insisted that local media be apprised immediately of the situation and what the company was doing about it, the story remained under control. The company signaled that it was more important to it to accept responsibility and do something about the crisis than to stop to figure out whether real "blame" lay with the builder of the storage tank, or the manufacturer of the steel from which it was constructed. By keeping the media informed, Ashland was able to limit conjecture and rumor and reduce the avalanche of criticism that such a significant oil spill would normally produce.

The moral of that story is that the public and the media will accept that "stuff" happens. How an organization responds when the stuff hits the fan will determine how it is judged—in the press and in the court of public opinion.

2. Consider timing issues.

Avoiding the media may work sometimes, but in a time of crisis, it won't work for long. The press can find too many other sources of information, many of whom may be more than happy for the media exposure, such as: disgruntled employees, state environmental officials, or your competitors. However, occasionally avoiding calls may be an appropriate short-term strategy—and the best way to temporarily delay media contact is to issue a "holding statement."

When to use a "holding statement":   Consider these two examples:

- *Scenario One:* You're planning an important formal announcement detailing the settlement you've reached with the EPA regarding a waste-water issue. But while details are being sorted through, and until all the pieces are put in place for an orderly communications program, you know that rumors have gotten to the local press. You may get calls from the media, calls that you can't reasonably ignore for days and days. If you did ignore them, it would become a sign that something is wrong.

- *Scenario Two:* You are preparing to make a major announcement in the morning—your company will be acquiring another firm. The announcement is timed to coincide with a legal filing, and you intend to coordinate communications with your employees, investors, customers, and other audiences. Yet you've received a phone message from a reporter covering your industry; she's heard speculation concerning your company's expansion plans. Not returning the reporter's call seems to be your only option.

For times like these, you'll need a "holding statement" that doesn't misrepresent current circumstances and provides enough information to fend off additional questions. This statement attempts to put the most positive face to the short-term situation, and sets the stage for later announcements, without prematurely revealing information. Crafting the statement and determining when to use it are key elements of crisis planning. Of course, your legal department or outside counsel will usually need to approve the holding statement and plans for its use.

When to use "exclusives":   Granting an "exclusive"—that is, telling your story to one reporter before the general announcement—is a controversial tactic. The theory is that one journalist either knows you best or is more important to your key audiences. Therefore, giving this individual more access to the story (and perhaps to your executives) in advance of a general announcement will ensure more favorable or more complete coverage (i.e., more of your side will get into print.) This positive story, in theory, will drive the tone and content of coverage in the rest of the media.

Sometimes exclusive placement works. Other times, giving favored treatment to one media outlet will anger competitive media. This negative reaction may result in a backlash and a determination on their part to dig for the "real" story. The subsequent coverage may show you in a worse light than if you had simply held the information and given everyone an equal shot at the news itself, even if you later chose to allow some more access to your executives.

3. Choose your communication channels.

From one-on-one conversation over the telephone to an electronically delivered press release, the channel you choose should achieve a specific communication objective. This basic tenet of communication strategy applies especially to channel choice during a crisis. (See pages 12–23 for a description of these channels and pages 41–52 for tips on how to use them.) The most commonly employed channels in a crisis are:

- Press release
- Telephone interview
- Press briefing
- Media availability
- Press conference
- Analyst conference call
- Corporate advertising
- Third-party support
- Video news release

Timing will play a role in channel choice. You will also need to consider how interactive the communication should be. And of course, you will need to assess the advantages and disadvantages of each option.

A good rule of thumb against which to measure your crisis response is to take what we call "The *60 Minutes* Test," named after the granddaddy of all investigative television programs. Answer three questions: What did you know? When did you know about it? What did you do once you knew about it? Acknowledging an appropriate level of responsibility and helping to drive toward solutions is the best way to pass this "test" and to win acquittal in the court of public opinion.

Providing timely information, avoiding an information vacuum, working with the media: as difficult or risky as these actions may seem, they offer better hope for favorable coverage in the long run.

When it comes to reminding the public of alleged or actual corporate errors, missteps, or misdeeds, the media suffer no amnesia. As a Native American proverb instructs: "Don't shoot an arrow that will return against you."

We hope we have provided a set of practical guidelines that will help you as you work with the media. We also hope that this book will give you a deeper understanding of how the media operates: what motivates the press, why reporters write certain kinds of stories, why they ask specific types of questions, and how media outlets determine which stories they will run. In turn, we hope that in the future you will be better prepared to control your relations with the media and effectively convey the messages that you want your audience to receive.

Bibliography

Books

Argenti, P., *Corporate Communication*, 2nd ed. New York: McGraw-Hill, 1998.

Argenti, P. and J. Forman, *The Power of Corporate Communication*. New York: McGraw-Hill, 2002.

Carlson, G., *Total Exposure*. New York: Amacom, 2000.

Croteau, D., Examining the "Liberal Media" Claim: Journalists' Views on Politics, Economic Policy and Media Coverage, FAIR Report, 1998.

Ewen, S., *PR! A Social History of Spin*. New York: Basic Books, 1996.

Fombrun, C., *Reputation*. Boston: Harvard Business School Press, 1996.

Harper, C., *And That's the Way It Will Be*. New York and London: New York University Press, 1998.

Hilton, J., *How to Meet the Press: A Survival Guide*. New York: Dodd, Mead & Company, 1987.

Horton, J., *Integrating Corporate Communications*. Connecticut and London: Quorum Books, 1995.

Jones, C., *Winning with the News Media*. Tampa: Video Consultants, Inc., 1999.

Kovach B. and T. Rosentiel, *Warp Speed: America in the Age of Mixed Media*. New York: Century Foundation Press, 1999.

Lerbinger, O., *The Crisis Manager: Facing Risk and Responsibility.* Mahwah, NJ: Lawrence Erlbaum Associates, 1997.

Ogrizek, M. and J. Guillery, *Communication in Crisis.* New York: Aldine de Gruyter, 1999.

Roberts, S., J. Frenette, and D. Stearns, *A Comparison of Media Outlets and Owners for Ten Selected Markets: 1960, 1980, 2000.* Media Bureau, Federal Communications Commission, October 2002.

Winter, M. and U. Steger, *Managing Outside Pressure: Strategies for Preventing Corporate Disasters.* New York: John Wiley & Sons, 1998.

Websites

www.fcc.org The Federal Communications Commission maintains a comprehensive website featuring ongoing research into current issues concerning the media.

www.niri.org The site of the National Investor Relations Institute, the authoritative professional association of corporate officers and investor relations consultants.

www.prsa.org The Public Relations Society of America offers a range of material of interest to all media relations practitioners on its website.

www.sec.gov The U.S. Securities and Exchange Commission provides vital information for anyone working in financial communication.

Index